WICKED
NORTH
ALABAMA

JACQUELYN PROCTER REEVES

THE
History
PRESS

Published by The History Press
Charleston, SC 29403
www.historypress.net

Copyright © 2009 by Jacquelyn Procter Reeves
All rights reserved

First published 2009
Second printing 2010
Third printing 2011
Fourth printing 2011
Fifth printing 2012

Manufactured in the United States

ISBN 978.1.59629.753.1

Library of Congress Cataloging-in-Publication Data

Reeves, Jacquelyn Procter.
Wicked North Alabama / Jacquelyn Procter Reeves.
p. cm.
ISBN 978-1-59629-753-1
1. Crime--Alabama--Case studies. 2. Murder--Alabama--Case studies. 3. Criminals--
Alabama--Case studies. I. Title.
HV6793.A2R44 2009
364.109761'9--dc22
2009033684

To my husband, Robert Reeves.

CONTENTS

PREFACE

The beauty of North Alabama and the generations of cultured hospitality take many people by surprise when they have occasion to visit. It is not the home of backward hillbillies as is sometimes portrayed by Hollywood, yet the residents of Alabama are in no hurry to change that image for fear of an invasion by those who are not like-minded. It is a peaceful, friendly, historic and progressive area of the South. Members of the Daughters of the American Revolution or United Daughters of the Confederacy now fight battles as courtroom lawyers, and southern English is spoken among rocket scientists. Still, North Alabama retains the charm and folksiness that make people want to invite neighbors over to eat pecan pie and watch the fireflies while remembering "back when."

Occasionally, the idyllic lives of these civic-minded people are interrupted by the tragic consequences of greed, lust, revenge and murder. Details are discussed at the beauty parlor, in the gyms and at the downtown cafés. These are the stories that inspire movies and songs. Some crimes remain officially unsolved, though the killers are known to one and all, and others continue to make the news decades later.

Many people have gone out of their way to help me find the interesting details that make these stories so memorable: Ranée Pruitt, Thomas Hutchens, Judge Bill Page, former district attorney Fred Simpson, Chuck and Jo Schaffer, Jim and Linda Maples, Jere Trent, Jerry Knight, Beverly Jolly, Dr. Pete Sparks, Charles (Chuck) Rice and Susanna Leberman. Thank you to all of these people and to my husband, Robert Reeves, who travels with me through crime scenes and cemeteries, archives and police stations, in order to feed my obsession with leaving no stone unturned. Robert is truly my partner in crime.

Road Gang Murder

Johnny Beecher was born in Wetumpka, Alabama, in 1933 to a mother who later died of syphilis. His father, who was not married to his mother, was a convicted murderer, adding yet another strike against him. Johnny was from a poor black family, and like most folks born into poverty, any hope of a promising future was a dream that belonged to others. People of all races in his socioeconomic situation simply existed, until the day they died.

When he was thirteen, Johnny moved to Buffalo, New York, to live with his father, but while there, he was arrested for stealing a bike. At some point, he was placed into foster care. Johnny was examined by doctors who diagnosed him as mentally unstable. In addition, he was a deviate and tortured his foster brother repeatedly, sexually and otherwise. When he returned to Alabama, Johnny was arrested for burglary. By the young age of seventeen, he had become fully entrenched in a long and extensive life of crime and imprisonment. He escaped from prison several times, adding more time onto each sentence. He had already been in and out of prison several times when he raped a woman in Clarke County in 1960. It looked like Johnny would spend his life in the Alabama prison system, but things were about to go from bad to worse.

In February 1964, Johnny Beecher was sent to Camp Scottsboro, where prisoners worked in the daytime and slept at night in a makeshift compound surrounded by a barbed-wire fence. The prison road gangs, not to be confused with chain gangs, were sent to help implement improvements in rural Jackson County, where residents lacked such luxuries as telephones, indoor plumbing and paved roads.

Martha Jane Chisenall. *Fred Simpson collection.*

The residents who lived around Camp Scottsboro appreciated the work of the men in the road gangs, as well they should have. They welcomed the arrival of improvements already enjoyed by their urban friends and appreciated the labors of the incarcerated men. The good folks of Jackson County also felt sorry for the men, who suffered through long days of hard labor in the elements, and frequently gave them something cool to drink, a pack of cigarettes or a friendly word. In fact, in many rural parts of Alabama, it was customary for a smoker to toss out what was left of his or her pack of cigarettes as he or she drove past the prisoners swinging sling blades from side to side to cut the weeds away from the roads and railroads.

Martha Jane Humphreys Chisenall was one of the residents whose kindness to the prisoners was well known. Occasionally, she gave them soda, cold milk or cookies, and even on the days when she had nothing to offer, she never failed to wave or smile. She would often see the prisoners when she was hanging laundry or sitting on her porch. One in particular seemed to be studying Martha, unbeknownst to her.

Johnny Beecher had been watching Martha ever since he first arrived at Camp Scottsboro. He talked about the "pretty young white woman" with the other convicts and told them he thought she liked him. He would look in the direction of her house at night and wonder what she was doing. He made one comment to another prisoner in early June 1964 that seemed somewhat odd. Perhaps he was thinking aloud when he said, "That scroungy bitch in that house is not worth dying for." He also said that she appeared to be "afflicted or messed up on one side."

Martha Chisenall was born in Cleveland, Tennessee. She had polio when she was young and it left lasting effects on her body. Her left hand was drawn, and at one time she had worn a brace. Pictures of Martha reveal a very attractive young woman with a sly grin and a twinkle in her blue eyes. Martha and her husband, Raymond Chisenall, were married in the Jackson County Courthouse on November 22, 1963. Sadly, the day of their celebration was a traumatic one for the nation; it was the day of President Kennedy's assassination. The Chisenalls lived near the River Road in Jackson County in a small rental house owned by Beulah Roper. The pretty country home had a front porch, two bedrooms and a kitchen.

On the morning of June 15, 1964, the hot sun rose early in the Alabama sky. The crickets' nocturnal songs quieted as the sun ascended. As they stopped chirping with the early morning light, the quiet peace was replaced with the clicking sound of cicadas, each competing to be heard over all others. It was the week before the official beginning of summer, but the temperature outside indicated that it had already arrived. Martha had fixed an enormous breakfast for her husband, a logger, and kissed him goodbye as he left for work shortly after 6:00 a.m.

Martha was wearing shorts and a checked shirt, and she had three rings on her fingers, including her high school graduation ring. She had just found out that she was two to three months pregnant. Martha was excited, and though she was only twenty-one years old, she knew that she had plenty of extended family to guide her through the struggles of parenthood. She placed her hand over her stomach and smiled.

Camp Scottsboro prisoners were loaded up at 6:00 a.m. for a day of work on the road. On this day, they were assigned to the River Road, which went to Coon Creek on Highway 117 at Stevenson near the Snodgrass Bridge. By 6:45 a.m., the seven members of the road gang were already hard at work moving fence posts so that highway workers could come in and prepare the dirt road for paving.

Johnny Beecher was two weeks away from his thirty-first birthday and serving a ten-year sentence for burglary and rape. He made small talk with another prisoner, Eddie Cooper, about the young white woman who lived in the nearby house. Beecher said he thought she liked him because she would wave and give him food. He wanted to go see her. He was obsessed with her.

Beecher was told to get fence posts by the captain of his team, Claude Sisk. The posts were located behind a barn. Mr. Sisk did not know it at the

Left: Johnny Beecher's mug shot. *Fred Simpson collection.*

Below: The Chisenall home. *Fred Simpson collection.*

time, but Beecher had come to a decision the night before. On Monday, June 15, Johnny Beecher planned to escape as soon as the opportunity presented itself. Perhaps he had another plan as well.

Beecher walked to the back of the barn where the fence posts were stacked, as he was told to do. He looked around to make sure that no one was watching him. Claude Sisk had turned his attention elsewhere, and the time had come to make his escape. Beecher began to run. He doubled back behind the house where the others were working and darted into the woods for cover. Nearby, he saw the back of the small wood-shingled rental home where Martha was alone.

Beecher cautiously came out of the woods and approached the house. In his pocket was a foot-long file that he had sharpened into a knife. He needed some clothes into which he could change and to get rid of his white prison shirt and pants with the number "58" stenciled on them. It was 7:15 a.m. when Beecher knocked on the back door of the home and tried to open the screen door, only to discover that it was locked.

Martha Chisenall unlocked the screen door and pushed it open. Beecher quickly slipped inside, and Martha realized her mistake. But it was too late. She screamed, and Beecher warned her to be quiet. He said that all he wanted were clothes so he could escape. She continued to scream, and he clapped his hand over her mouth. He told her that he wouldn't hurt her if she would just stop yelling. He took his hand off her mouth and she screamed again. Beecher threw Martha to the floor and told her that he hadn't planned to rape her, but since she was causing him trouble, he might as well do it. He figured that he would be accused of the crime whether he committed it or not.

Beecher dragged Martha into the adjacent bedroom and pulled his knife out so she could see it. He threw her on the bed and removed her clothing from the waist down. Beecher placed the knife on her shoulder with the blade facing her neck so she would know that it wouldn't take much for him to quickly stab her.

Martha locked her eyes on the ceiling as Beecher raped her, hoping that he would get it over with and leave. But when he finished, he ordered her off the bed and told her to put on her clothes and shoes.

Meanwhile, the captain of the work detail, Claude Sisk, realized that Beecher was gone. He yelled for Beecher to come back and walked up into the woods to yell again. A sick feeling came over him. Sisk loaded the remaining prisoners into the truck and took them back to Camp Scottsboro. He went to nearby homes to warn the residents that Beecher was loose and possibly dangerous. Sisk knocked on the door of the Chisenall home, but there was no answer. He heard a radio playing loudly inside the home, and after he knocked, the radio was turned down. Sisk did not go in, even though the door was unlocked. He later said that he was afraid Mrs. Chisenall might be naked. As he turned to leave, the volume was turned up again. Sisk went to Jack Cableton's store to summon help on his shortwave radio.

Beecher was alone again with Martha. He ripped a strip of the sheet from the bed and used it as a gag. He then tied her hands behind her back. She quietly followed his orders, and with him behind her, she stepped outside the house. Martha walked in front of Beecher as he held onto her hands behind her back. They stepped over a wood fence behind the house and walked toward the woods. As they continued, they stopped twice for Martha to rest. Before long, they came to an empty house on the mountaintop. Beecher ordered Martha inside, and then he raped her again.

Beecher forced Martha out of the abandoned building and headed in the direction of a strip mine near Fabius. The noise of loud machines filled the air, and large trucks loaded with coal passed on the road. They walked in the direction of the mine, but outside of anyone's sight. Down below the mine, Beecher took off his shirt and tore it into strips. He blindfolded Martha and tied a strip across her nose and around her ankles. Then he took off his tan belt and secured it around her neck. He tightened it until it began to strangle her. Though her mouth was gagged, she was making noise. Beecher took a handful of dirt and forced it into her mouth. The pretty young wife suffered a slow, merciless death. It took close to nine minutes for her to lose consciousness and give up her struggle to live.

Beecher picked up Martha's limp body and found a shallow depression in the ground. He doubled her over into the fetal position, leaving her hands tied behind her back. He covered her with dirt and leaves and dragged a rotten log on top of her. He took the rest of his torn shirt, including the collar stamped with the number "58," and buried it in a small hole next to Martha's makeshift grave. Beecher looked down at the ground above Martha's body for a while to make sure there was no movement. The time was about 5:30 p.m.

Beecher headed toward Highway 117 and crossed it near a tall tower. He passed Jack Cableton's store and found a place in the woods behind a trailer house where he slept, knowing that authorities would already be looking for him.

Raymond Chisenall's father was plowing cotton about midmorning when a guard drove up and told him that a prisoner had escaped from the road gang. The guard told him to take his clothes off the clothesline and remove his keys from his car's ignition. Mr. Chisenall then rode his tractor out into the field, where his thirteen-year-old son and eighteen-year-old daughter were picking cotton. He told them to go into the house for safety, but first they were to get Martha from her home and bring her in for safety, too. The two teenagers were near Martha's house when they heard the radio playing loudly from inside. It was too loud. They hollered at Martha but got no answer. The door was ajar. They walked inside and found the refrigerator door open and food lying on the floor as if it had been pitched out in a hurry. It wasn't like Martha to do that, and certainly she would not have the music on as loud as the knob would go. The rest of the house was in disarray as well. In addition, they discovered a piece of paper, on which Martha had hastily scribbled the word "convict." Raymond Chisenall's sister ran out to get Mrs. Roper, who lived down the road, and when she returned, they summoned the police. Martha and Beecher had not been gone very long.

Raymond was located at work and brought home to look for anything out of place that might help the authorities find Martha. He was upset and could not help. When Raymond left the house that day, he never went back. About one thousand armed men, women and even some children combed the north side of Sand Mountain in search of the escaped convict, hoping that he had just taken Martha hostage and she was still alive. Soon they found two sets of footprints, and their hopes were renewed. The footprints indicated that at times Martha was walking and at times she was dragged. The larger footprints were examined, and they appeared to belong to someone wearing prison-issued slip-bottom brogans. News crews arrived at the Chisenall house and set up cameras. Bloodhounds were brought in, along with their trainers from Draper Prison, and quickly picked up a scent until a helicopter flew overhead and scattered the dogs in different directions. It took an hour to gather them together, and by then the dogs had lost the scent. Crucial time was lost as the trainers got them back on the trail.

The next morning the search continued. At about 9:40 a.m., Herbert Acker, with the Cherokee County Rescue Squad, looked under some brush and saw that leaves and dirt had been disturbed. Green flies were swarming all around. He called for help and began to dig. Acker found Martha's body in its shallow grave, with the belt still wrapped around her neck and her hands still bound behind her back. One of the strips of binding bore the words "Alabama Board of Corrections." They also found the remnants of Beecher's shirt nearby. It was obvious that Martha had been sexually molested. Her clothing was ripped, and there were bite marks all over her body. "There was no cause to kill a pregnant woman for sex. That's all it was," Acker said.

When word got out that she had been found, Raymond, who was understandably distraught, was not allowed to make the identification. Martha's brother, twenty-six-year-old Johnny Humphrey, was summoned to her shallow grave to identify her. He brushed dirt off her, wrapped his arms around her body and wondered how he would give their mother the horrible news.

Within minutes, the bloodhounds arrived at the grave site. When the convicts who had trained the dogs saw that Martha was dead, they were furious. They didn't waste any time getting back on the trail, but it was different now. This time they were looking for a killer.

Martha's mother and sister, both of whom had been waiting impatiently in Tennessee since the day before, decided to drive down to Martha's house and wait there. As they turned onto the road that led to her house, the ambulance slowly pulled out—and they knew. News of Martha's death spread quickly. The posse of several hundred armed men, their anger fueled by the promise of revenge, continued the manhunt. It was understood, without being spoken, that Beecher would not be brought in alive.

Early the following morning, Wednesday, June 17, Beecher found a boat belonging to Cicero Payne chained to roots on the riverbank. He crossed the Tennessee River in the boat, using a board he found in the boat as a paddle. While he was on the water, he took Martha's three gold rings out of his right front pocket and threw them into the river, perhaps hoping not to implicate himself in her disappearance. When he got to shore, he began to walk along the railroad tracks. Late that afternoon, he took a shirt off a clothesline and hid for several hours near a cement plant. Beecher walked into a grocery store in Richard City, Tennessee, with blood and mud on him. The woman who took his money for hot dogs and bread looked down at the blood. She knew, from bulletins that had run all day, that a convict was loose and the body of a young pregnant woman had been found. Even more suspicious was that the man before her wore glasses with no lenses. He handed her a one-dollar silver certificate and she gave him change. As soon as he was gone, she told her husband that the convict who killed the Alabama woman had just left the store. They notified the police.

Beecher hid near the railroad depot that night, knowing that the police and somewhat hysterical civilian posses were looking for him. Just before daylight, he made his way along the tracks and saw the police. At just after 4:00 a.m., he ran across a field. Connie Mack Barnes, a twenty-eight-year-old South Pittsburg, Tennessee police officer, shot Beecher in the knee with his .30-30 rifle. With a pistol and a rifle pressed against his head, Beecher admitted he had killed Martha Chisenall and begged Officer Barnes not to turn him over to the mob in Stevenson.

The community breathed a sigh of relief that a killer had been caught. Beecher was taken to South Pittsburg Municipal Hospital, where he received medical treatment. Several days later, his leg, which had turned gangrenous, was amputated.

An autopsy was performed on Martha's body by State Toxicologist Vann Pruitt the day after it was found. It revealed what they already suspected: Martha had been raped and beaten, and the official cause of death was strangulation. Although tests concluded that she had been pregnant, the fetus was no longer present at the time of the autopsy.

On June 22, Beecher dictated a twenty-two-page confession over the course of five hours. At the conclusion of his statement, he said, "It wasn't my intentions to harm her but the way it turned out was the way it was meant to be. Even though I killed her it wasn't my intentions to." Later, Beecher claimed that his physical and mental conditions were not good and that he had given the confession involuntarily; furthermore, he claimed that he was innocent of both the rape and murder of Martha Chisenall.

Beecher's trial took place in the Jackson County Courthouse in Scottsboro on September 21, 1964. His court-appointed attorneys were Joe Lee, Jim McGintey and Andy Hamlett. Prosecutors were John T. Black and Bob Thomas. Nearly one thousand people attended the trial, which was kept in order by a large number of officers scattered throughout the crowd. On September 22, the jury took just over an hour to find Beecher guilty and sentence him to death. Beecher showed no emotion, and the crowd did not utter a sound as the sentence was announced. Judge Jack Livingston scheduled Johnny Daniel Beecher, alias Johnnie Johnson, alias Johnny Duke, to die on January 2, 1965. Before the sentence could be carried out, Justice Hugo Black ordered a stay of execution, pending a review of the case after Beecher claimed that he had been ordered to confess at the time he had been shot. Regarding the second confession he made several days later, Beecher said that he was under the influence of drugs and in considerable pain.

In October 1967, the conviction was overturned. The U.S. Supreme Court ruled that the confession was obtained through gross coercion, and Beecher would be tried again. Circuit court judge John Proctor agreed to the defense's request for a mental evaluation. The three-member commission ruled that Johnny Beecher was sane at the time he was admitted to Searcy Hospital for his sanity hearing, and furthermore, he had been sane at the time he committed the crime.

In December 1971, the Supreme Court ordered a new trial. The second trial was held in the Cherokee County town of Centre, and Judge Newton Powell presided. On February 5, 1969, Beecher was found guilty a second time, but once again, the conviction was overturned because his attorney argued that the first confession had been forced out of him at gunpoint and the second confession coerced out of him while he was under the influence of pain killers. The third trial, originally scheduled for Cherokee County, was moved to the Lawrence County town of Moulton because a jury could not be impaneled. Although it was scheduled to begin on March 12, a continuation was granted because witness Claude Sisk was hospitalized in Jackson County. On June 18, 1973, nine years and three days after the murder of Martha Chisenall, the third trial began in Moulton. On June 21, Beecher was found guilty for a third time, but the conviction was overturned because the prosecutor, DeKalb County district attorney John Black, made a remark about Beecher not taking the stand in his defense. Mr. Black asked to be replaced as prosecutor.

In the meantime, a newspaper article in July 1978 revealed that Beecher had been held in a minimum-security prison and was sent to work-release assignments.

Beecher's attorneys wanted him released on the grounds that a fourth trial over the course of twelve years violated his right to a speedy and fair trial. An NAACP attorney said that Beecher should have been released upon the expiration of his 1964 sentence and that he had been illegally locked up for seven years beyond the time of his previous sentence. The NAACP representative complained that Kilby Prison was overcrowded, the facilities were dilapidated and living conditions were bad, and because of "rampant violence and a jungle atmosphere," prisoners had to carry weapons to protect themselves. Additionally, Beecher's attorneys asked that he be released on bail.

Special prosecutor Fred Simpson, Madison County district attorney, was assigned by Attorney General Bill Baxley to fight for the state in Beecher's fourth trial. He had to go to New Orleans and argue the case before the Fifth

Circuit to get permission to proceed. It was granted. Simpson knew that this would probably be the last chance to get a solid conviction, and he could not introduce Beecher's confession as evidence against him. Still, the severity of the crime warranted at least one more attempt.

Beecher was represented by Jerry Knight, a court-appointed attorney from Decatur. Judge Newton Powell would preside again. Finally, on May 1, 1979, Beecher entered a plea of not guilty, and on May 14, the fourth trial began in Moulton. The jury was sequestered in Decatur.

This trial was different from the three previous trials. Although it had been fifteen years since Martha's murder, the prosecution contacted all of the witnesses it could find to testify. Some remembered the incident like it was yesterday; others were a little vague in their recollections. Prosecutors in the previous cases had not called many witnesses, assuming that they weren't needed, but at this time, without benefit of the confessions, prosecutors wanted to make sure there was not a shred of doubt left in the minds of the jurors when they left the room to deliberate. Martha's husband testified, as did her sister. They even found the convict who had handled the dogs.

After fifteen years, the dog handler was back in prison. Convicts who had served time with Beecher and heard him comment about Martha testified against him, as did witnesses who saw him dragging Martha while she was bound. Another witness was Officer Barnes, who put the bullet in Beecher's leg at the time he was caught. Simpson asked the officer why he shot Beecher in the leg instead of the torso. Barnes answered simply that he couldn't bring himself to kill him.

Although it had been fifteen years since Martha's death, her brother, Johnny Humphrey, sobbed during his testimony. He described his reaction when he arrived at his sister's shallow grave: "I wrapped my arms around her and thought 'I've got to go tell Mother.'"

During the trial, prosecutor Fred Simpson told the jury that Beecher "had confessed to everybody who would listen to him…I don't think there is a jury in the country who would believe that it is a coincidence that a convict runs away from a road gang and the next day a woman is found murdered and bound with strips stamped Department of Corrections." In his closing remarks, he said, "If you want to tell him what you think about what he did, come back and give him 1,000 years in the penitentiary. That would be a nice little message."

On Wednesday, May 16, Beecher was convicted for a fourth time, and again, he did not take the witness stand. His conviction for first-degree murder automatically gave him life in prison.

Johnny Daniel Beecher has been denied parole numerous times. He is presently incarcerated at Kilby Prison, with no release date. In the end, there were many "what ifs?" What if the people who saw Beecher drag Martha Chisenall across the road and through the woods had been able to telephone police? What if the helicopter had not disturbed the tracking dogs, who were possibly within minutes of finding Martha? And finally, what if the bullet that had passed through Beecher's knee had gone through his chest instead?

The murder of Martha Chisenall forever changed the prison system. Within days of her disappearance, a new ruling was issued that no prisoner with a criminal background of rape or molestation would ever be assigned to another road gang. Because this happened when the civil rights movement was beginning to gain momentum, the NAACP and others used this ruling as a forum to claim that Beecher was discriminated against because of his racial background. No doubt that pervasive argument played heavily into the reversal of his conviction on three occasions. But Martha Chisenall is still dead, a casualty of one of the most heinous crimes in Alabama history.

THE PERFECT CRIME

Just outside Fayetteville, Tennessee, lies the peaceful Riverview Cemetery. The hills roll gracefully, and here and there a bouquet of silk flowers adds color to a weathered gravestone. Brian Scott, a former deputy with the Madison County Sheriff's Department, is the caretaker of the serene burial ground. Mr. Scott has experienced strange incidents during the many solitary hours he spends at Riverview. Fleeting shadows and darting images of people catch his peripheral vision and pass behind him quickly, only to disappear and leave him wondering if his imagination is playing tricks on him. Sometimes a particular gravestone will suddenly shine brightly, while others around it remain in the shadows, only to resume the quiet countenance it bore moments before. He knows his "residents" well, however. On a recent spring morning, two visitors asked about the location of a murder victim's grave, and in spite of the twenty-five acres of headstones, Mr. Scott took them immediately to the spot they were looking for. As a cold gust of wind blew over the hills, the story of the grave at their feet unfolded.

On Friday, May 28, 1976, Judy Alter answered the telephone at her home on Rustic Circle in Southeast Huntsville. It was just after eight o'clock in the morning; her children were at school, and her husband was at work. Despite it being late spring, it was drizzling and gloomy outside. The thirty-six-year-old willowy brunette was still wearing her nightgown as she settled down for a comfortable telephone conversation with her lover. Who knows what they discussed that morning. She had approached her husband the evening before to discuss their marital troubles. She had been distant lately and brought up the subject of divorce. Perhaps she revealed to her husband that she was seeing someone else.

Her call was interrupted by a knock on the door. Judy told the caller to hold on while she answered the door. She laid down the phone and never picked it up again.

Judy answered the door, and her guest, holding a knife, stepped inside. Together they went to the upstairs bathroom. Judy was instructed to remove her nightgown.

The uninvited guest that day was the wife of Judy's lover. At age forty-eight, "the other woman" was some twelve years older than Judy and average looking, perhaps even matronly. More importantly, she was the scorned woman. In the bathroom, the older woman raised her arm, knife in hand, and slashed at her husband's younger lover. She kept slashing, stabbing, cutting and gouging. No doubt Judy screamed, but there was no one to hear her cry out for help. Ribbons of blood splashed the walls as the killer raised her arm time and time again. As Judy slumped to the ground, her killer continued to plunge the knife into her. Judy raised her arms defensively to shield herself but finally collapsed into the bathtub, unconscious. Within moments, the blood that had gushed from her wounds faded to a trickle. Judy's breathing, and her struggle to live, stopped. The killer left.

At 11:16 a.m., Judy's lover drove to her house, worried because she had not returned to the phone. He went inside and was horrified to find that she had been savagely murdered. He called the police, and within minutes the cul-de-sac was filled with investigators. Coroner Sam Spry examined the nude body of Judy Alter, lying face up in the bathtub. She had been dead several hours. He made a quick assessment and announced, to no one's surprise, that the death of Mrs. Alter was definitely a homicide. He said that the victim had been stabbed at least eighteen to twenty times, but his first estimate was low. She had been stabbed an unbelievable twenty-eight times, though the newspaper would later report forty-four stab wounds.

Judy's lover was questioned, as was Judy's husband. They were both cleared. But something caused the police to look at the lover's wife. Did he reveal his suspicions about his wife to the police? Police went to the lover's home on Trousdale Street to see what they could find. They saw something right away that looked out of place. The woman had clothing hanging out on the clothesline to dry. They were her clothes, including her tennis shoes. They had been washed that morning, in fact, and now they were on the clothesline—in the rain.

A knife was found in the kitchen with blood on it. The woman had blood under her fingernails, too, but she explained that she had just cut up a chicken. She had rented a car from Woody Anderson Ford that

The home where Judy Alter was murdered. *Photograph by Robert Reeves.*

The killer's clothes hanging up to dry.

morning while hers was in the shop for repairs. The mileage on the rental car coincided exactly with the route she would have taken to the Alter home. After the suspect had been questioned thoroughly, the police knew they had their killer, but in the days before sophisticated forensics, there simply wasn't enough evidence—yet—to bring her before a grand jury. In addition, she refused to take a lie detector test.

District Attorney Fred Simpson knew he had to move cautiously. If the suspect was indicted for murder, she could demand a speedy trial, yet there wasn't enough evidence to ensure a conviction. If she were tried and found not guilty, she could never be tried again, even if the proof that would cinch her conviction came later. Simpson decided to wait.

Meanwhile, Judy Alter's funeral service was held the following Monday at St. Stephens Episcopal Church. "She was a real nice, decent person... kind of a loner, but real nice," one neighbor was quoted as saying. Judy's body was taken to Riverview Cemetery in Fayetteville, Tennessee, for burial. In lieu of flowers, the family requested that money be donated to several named charities. In July, less than two months later, her husband sold the home on Rustic Circle and moved with his children to California, where he accepted a transfer with his job. He wanted to get as far away from the pain as he could and perhaps save his children from further trauma. But like the police, he also knew who had killed his wife.

Less than three weeks after the gruesome murder, the killer filed for divorce from her husband on the grounds of adultery. He had already moved out of the family home on Trousdale Street, perhaps immediately, in fear for his own life. She had killed his lover and now she wanted to destroy him through the legal system.

Divorce records indicate that they had been married for twenty-five years and had one teenaged son. She was twenty-three years old when they were married; he had just turned twenty-one. Both were college graduates, but because she had very little work experience, and none in the previous few years, she wanted the home, as well as spousal support. He helped compile a list of questions that his attorney would ask her in a deposition, including details about her hospitalization, two days before the murder, for an apparent overdose of tranquilizers.

As the weeks dragged into months, her urgency for a divorce settlement increased. It was his wish that details of their marital discord (and perhaps her secret?) be kept out of the records to shield their son. When it was finally settled, she was awarded the family home and $350 per month until she married or until her death. Her ex-husband was awarded custody of their child.

The victim's grave in Fayetteville, Tennessee. *Photograph by Robert Reeves.*

The now yellowed pages of the 1976 *Huntsville Times* tell the story of the May 28 murder of a young mother of three. The article went on to say that Judy was stabbed while cornered in the bathroom. Police expected to make an arrest "any day." But time continued to pass. The years rolled into decades. In spite of what was considered common knowledge of the identity of the murderer, there has never been enough evidence to bring her to justice. With no statute of limitations on murder, the case remains open and, technically, unsolved.

Now, it is finally too late. Twenty-eight years after Judy's death, the last person she spoke to, besides her killer, died in the summer of 2004. Judy's lover had remarried, and, as one would expect, his son was listed among his next of kin. He was a member of St. Stephens Episcopal Church.

In the cold winter of 2007, Judy Alter's killer died. She had never moved away from the house where she washed her bloody clothing and hung it up in the rain, nor had she remarried. Her only child was not listed among the next of kin, and like her former husband and Judy Alter, she was a member of St. Stephens Episcopal Church. Perhaps it was their church affiliation—the one common denominator—that facilitated their fateful clash with destiny.

WICKED WOMEN
THE SCOTTSBORO BOYS INCIDENT

It was March 25, 1931, in Scottsboro, Alabama. Two women dressed in coveralls—vagabonds really—were among a group that stepped off a freight train. They tried to melt into the crowd that had gathered, but someone stopped them. The tale they told that day ensured that, within a few short days, their names would be known all over the United States. It also sparked, according to some historians, the beginning of the civil rights movement.

Victoria Price was born in 1908 to sixty-two-year-old John Price and his thirty-eight-year-old wife, Ella. It was not Ella's first marriage and probably not John's either. John Price was a farmer, and the family lived on New Cut Road in Lincoln County, Tennessee. But John was dead within a few short years, and Victoria, her mother and her brothers, Shelby and Tillman, moved to Huntsville to find work in one of the many cotton mills. Victoria later claimed that she quit school at age ten to help support her mother.

According to the 1930 census, Ella Price, a fifty-five-year-old widow (her age disagrees with the dates on her headstone), lived at 313 Arms Street with her daughter, Victoria McClendon, who had married Enos McClendon on December 14, 1929. The marriage was short-lived, mostly because she shot him. This was her second failed marriage, although it did last a little longer than her first one. In 1927, she had married Henry Pressley, but according to Victoria, their wedded bliss lasted a whopping two and a half hours. Victoria was a rather plain, perhaps even harsh-looking young woman. Her lips were thin, and her narrowed eyes suggested a suspicious nature. Perhaps it was hard work in the cotton mills that caused her to look older than her age.

Margaret Mill. *Photograph courtesy of the Huntsville-Madison County Public Library.*

The Huntsville Cotton Mill opened on Jefferson Street in 1881, specializing in the production of soft-spun yarn. In 1918, the name of the steam-driven operation was changed to Margaret Mill. It was changed again in 1933 to Fletcher Mill. In its heyday, it employed over three hundred workers to keep ten thousand spindles humming. With the arrival of the union, employees who went on strike brought the mill to its knees. It closed in 1932 and was finally torn down in 1950. Victoria was a spinner at the Margaret Mill, and this was where she met a teenager named Ruby Bates, another spinner, who lived with her widowed mother, Emma, at 314 Grove Avenue.

Ruby's father, Ed Bates, died sometime prior to 1930, leaving his wife alone to raise Ruby, her younger sister Annie and her younger brother. At least one source claimed that Ed Bates was a violent alcoholic who took his rage out on his family. Emma Bates worked at the Margaret Mill as a winder. The two girls, Victoria and Ruby, had something else in common as well. During the Great Depression, their hours at the mill were not enough to keep the money coming in on a consistent basis. Both girls turned to prostitution to supplement their incomes.

The train tracks alongside the Huntsville Depot. *Photograph courtesy of the Huntsville-Madison County Public Library.*

Of the two, Victoria possessed a stronger personality, and Ruby oftentimes followed along with whatever Victoria told her to do. Victoria did not know where her estranged husband, Enos McClendon, was, but she heard that he was headed on to bigger and better things in New Orleans. Victoria already had another boyfriend, this one married, and she and Ruby had spent the night of March 23, 1931, in the company of Victoria's boyfriend and another young man.

On Tuesday, March 24, 1931, twenty-three-year-old Victoria Price and eighteen-year-old Ruby Bates hopped on a train. The two women wore coveralls over their dresses so that they could move about on the train even though they didn't have tickets. They were en route to Chattanooga, Tennessee, to see if they could find steady work at a mill there. Neither had been to Chattanooga, and they took with them only the name of Callie Brochie, who had a boardinghouse on Seventh Street where they could stay. They arrived in Chattanooga at 7:30 p.m., and Victoria asked a stranger if he knew where Mrs. Brochie lived. He told her that she lived in the fourth house on Seventh Street. Between 6:00 and 7:00 a.m. the next morning, they left the boardinghouse to visit the Thatcher Company Mill, hoping to get a job. They were hired, and at about noon, they hopped a freight train to return to Huntsville to gather up their belongings and head back north.

The train was slightly late getting out of the station. The conductor saw that there were a number of hobos on the train, but in an effort to make up for lost time, he decided, this time, to look the other way. On the train were a number of young white men traveling together and several young black men, some of whom were also traveling together.

It was late March, and bright yellow forsythia blooms reached their willowy arms upward in search of golden sunshine. But on that day, the temperature had not reached sixty degrees and the wind was blowing cold. Coupled with the speed of the train, the raw wind cut like a knife through the threadbare clothing worn by the hobos traveling in open cars. Soon after boarding the train, they all began to hop from one car to another to find the best place to wait out the ride. They ended up on a gondola car with about two feet of chert.

A fight broke out on the train near Stevenson; some of the white boys were pushed off the train, and others were forced to jump. Those who were pushed or fell went straight to authorities, who wired ahead to Scottsboro to stop the train. As the train pulled into the station, about fifteen deputized men ordered everyone off. Nine young black men climbed down from the train, along with two white women—Ruby Bates and Victoria Price. Ruby and Victoria tried to quietly slip away, but when they were stopped, Victoria panicked. She did not want to be arrested for vagrancy, so she contrived a way out. She pointed an accusatory finger at the young black men and said that she and Ruby had been gang raped by them.

In the 1930s, an accusation of this nature was tantamount to throwing gasoline onto a raging fire. The startled young men were promptly arrested and taken to jail. Judge Alred Hawkins presided over the grand jury, which voted to indict the nine young men, some of whom were mere boys, for rape. The judge appointed all seven of Scottsboro's attorneys to represent them, but six reported conflicts. One attorney claimed that because he represented the Alabama Power Company, his client stood to profit financially in the event that they were electrocuted.

A doctor testified that he had examined the girls after the incident and found evidence that they had had sex, but the sperm was nonmotile. In addition, there was no evidence that they had been mauled—no bruises, lacerations or tears. Ruby's examination showed that she had had sex with one man. Victoria also had sperm inside her, but there certainly was not enough to indicate that they had been gang raped.

Victoria's testimony was dramatic, wild and accented with inflammatory detail. To make matters worse, several of the young men, in an effort to save themselves, implicated one another. Within only a few weeks, the young men were all convicted and sentenced to die. But their attorney had a drinking problem, and fortunately for them, the suggestion that their attorney had not argued ably on their behalf helped persuade the U.S. Supreme Court to overturn the conviction. In addition, a change of venue was granted due to the widespread publicity.

In 1933, two years after their arrest, the young men, now known far and wide as the Scottsboro Boys, were sent to the Morgan County Courthouse in Decatur for their new trials. Judge James Edward Horton, a tall, well-educated native of Alabama, was assigned to preside over the trial by the chief justice of the Supreme Court. Judge Horton reserved seats for the out-of-town newspaper reporters, since by now the incident had attained international notoriety.

During or around the time of the trial, Victoria Price vanished. Rumors flew that she had been kidnapped—or worse. Sheriff Ben Giles was notified and immediately launched an investigation into her disappearance. As it turned out, she had accompanied her mother to Tennessee to fill out paperwork for a pension.

In the meantime, Ruby Bates changed her testimony and revealed that the entire story was a lie. She disappeared and then unexpectedly returned to Decatur to testify in the March trial of Haywood Patterson, the first of the Scottsboro Boys to go on trial. Ruby bore no resemblance to the poor millworker from two years earlier. Her clothes were stylish and new, and her manners were not quite as coarse as before. Her now former friend Victoria Price, angry at Ruby's change of story, clobbered her in the face with her purse when she saw her. Ruby testified that they had lied about the rapes, but Victoria continued to claim that it was all true. Victoria's answers, however, were vague and more than a little hostile. In the meantime, Victoria put the word out that she would change her testimony for a price. When a man arrived from New York with a bundle of cash, she promptly turned him in to authorities. The defense attorney cornered Victoria on her claim that they had stayed at a boardinghouse in Chattanooga after a man claimed that he had sex with one of the girls in what was known then as a "hobo jungle." Still, she did not back down on her story.

After the trial began, Judge Horton accidentally met up with one of the doctors who had examined the two women for evidence of rape. The doctor told the judge, confidentially, that there was no way that the women were forced to have sex, especially with multiple partners, but he was afraid that his testimony would end his career. The judge felt that twelve honest men would recognize the truth—the innocence of

Above, left: Ruby Bates on the witness stand.

Above, right: Victoria Price on the witness stand.

the Scottsboro Boys—and set them all free. He underestimated the jury however, and they came back with a verdict of guilty. The punishment was set at death.

Judge Horton carefully wrote his twenty-six-page brief to support the announcement he was about to make. The verdict was set aside. Judge Horton ordered another trial for Haywood Patterson and suspended the remaining trials until public outcry had settled down. Perhaps Judge Horton knew that this move would end his political career, but he never had a moment of regret. The new trials were conducted by Judge William Callahan, whose bias against Ruby Bates and the Scottsboro Boys was evident. Not surprisingly, they were all found guilty.

In early May 1933, three thousand people paraded in Washington, D.C., to bring to light the plight of the Scottsboro Boys and ask President Roosevelt to intervene. Among the marchers were Ruby Bates and the mother of Haywood Patterson. Ruby told every audience that would listen that neither she nor Victoria had been raped. President Roosevelt was unable to see them, and his representative told the marchers that it was a matter for the courts, not Congress. Sadly, no one, and nobody, could persuade the courts to let the young men go.

Haywood Patterson was tried four times and spent sixteen years in prison. He was released but got into a bar fight in 1950 and was arrested for murder when a man in the fight was killed. He was convicted of manslaughter in his third trial but died of cancer in 1952, less than one year after his return to prison.

Charles Weems, nineteen at the time of his arrest, was the oldest of the Scottsboro Boys. He was paroled in 1943 and moved to Atlanta, where he led a quiet life.

Clarence Norris was paroled in 1944 but violated his parole by moving out of state. He was arrested and paroled again. In 1976, he received a pardon from Alabama governor George Wallace. He died in New York in 1989 at age seventy-six, the last of the Scottsboro Boys to die.

Andy Wright, also nineteen at the time of his arrest, was paroled in 1944. He married that same year, but in violation of his parole, he left the state and was arrested and imprisoned again. He was released again in 1950 and was later accused of raping a thirteen-year-old girl, but this time he was acquitted by an all-white jury.

Ozie Powell was sixteen when he was arrested. He was shot in the head when he stabbed a deputy with a pen and sustained permanent brain damage. He was paroled in 1946 and moved back to Georgia.

Olen Montgomery was seventeen in 1931. He was released from prison in 1937 and bounced from one job to another, never staying at one for any period of time.

Thirteen-year-old Eugene Williams was released in July 1937.

Willie Roberson, seventeen in 1931, had an extremely painful case of syphilis at the time of the alleged rapes. He walked with a cane and was finally released in 1937, at which time he moved to New York.

Roy Wright, thirteen-year-old brother of Andy Wright, said that he saw the other boys rape the girls, hoping to gain his release. He was also released in 1937, joined the army and got married. His end was as tragic as his early life, however. In a jealous rage, he shot his wife to death and then killed himself in August 1952.

Ruby Bates toured the United States speaking for the International Labor Defense, which, along with the NAACP, helped fund the defense team for the Scottsboro Boys. In 1934, she went to work in New York in a spinning factory until she was diagnosed with tuberculosis. She returned to Huntsville and lived with her mother. Ruby Bates Schut died in 1976 in Washington. Only two days before her death, Alabama governor George Wallace pardoned Clarence Norris.

Victoria Price's grave in Fayetteville, Tennessee. *Photograph by Robert Reeves.*

In the 1940s, Victoria Price married, for a third time, a man named Frank Roland in Lincoln County, Tennessee. This marriage did not last, and she married a fourth and final time to Dean Street. Victoria Street died on October 17, 1982, in a Huntsville hospital at the age of seventy-seven. She was a resident of Corders Crossroads, near Flintville, Tennessee, in the years prior to her death. Victoria sued NBC over the movie *Judge Horton and the Scottsboro Boys*, which aired in 1976, claiming that it contained many lies about her. In court, she was seated, unbeknownst to any of them, next to two of Judge Horton's sons. The lawsuit was, at the very least, frivolous, but her attorneys, who hoped to make a name for themselves, pursued it with vigor. Although the lawsuit was dismissed from federal court, Victoria and her attorneys planned to file for another trial. The network decided that, rather than go through another expensive trial, it would offer a settlement after the U.S. Supreme Court announced it would review the case. Victoria said later that she was satisfied with the settlement and had used part of the money to buy her home.

Today, the Scottsboro Boys incident is recognized for what it really was: the senseless conviction of innocent young men whose lives were ruined by the accusations of two self-serving women caught up in the glamour of notoriety. The reputation of the state of Alabama was tainted, as was the career of Judge Horton. Yet the City of Scottsboro recognizes that the terrible truth, which will haunt the city until the end of time, should not be swept under the rug. On the lawn of the Jackson County Courthouse, a historical marker acknowledges the tragedy that will forever be known as the story of the Scottsboro Boys.

THE BUCK ISLAND MASSACRE

Ａmerica's War Between the States remains one of the most written about and discussed topics a century and a half after it ended. Rivers of blood, washed by the tears of those left behind, touched nearly every family in the nation. As in any war, scores of innocent lives were lost at the hands of devils, and some were forgotten in the endless list of atrocities. In too many cases, these people had no political affiliation and no stand to take. They only wanted to be left alone.

In December 1864, the war was winding down and the people of northern Alabama were weary. As the Confederacy realized that its resources were quickly running out, and it became apparent that its men were nearly all consigned to graveyards and battlefields, common sense dictated that the end was near. Plantation homes were abandoned or in ruins, leaving silent chimneys alone in fields near neglected family cemeteries. Businesses had been burned and crops destroyed by the Union army.

The Roden family of Marshall County, Alabama, was large in number, and except for a few members who fought for the Confederacy, they supported neither the North nor the South. It wasn't their war, and they had nothing at stake. But theirs was a story, like so many others, in which the War Between the States came to them.

Just outside the community of Guntersville, the Rodens hid their cattle from both armies on the Tennessee River island known as Buck Island. Though it no longer exists, it was, at one time, a wilderness that offered a safe haven for those who wished not to be found. It was named for an old stag that hid out in the dense canebrakes, safe from the many game hunters in the area. In the 1860s, oak, hickory and gum trees covered the eighty or so acres.

Like most recollections of long ago, details do not always agree. Such is the case with the following story. This event took place, according to some accounts, in 1863, and in others, 1864. For the purpose of simplicity, this version occurs in the year 1864, with the understanding that the actual date may not ever be positively known.

Benjamin Roden was a man of some sixty-eight years who possessed much native intelligence. He would sink his ferry out of sight in the water until he needed it, raise it back up, plug the holes so that it would float and then sink it again when he was finished with it. This kept his ferry out of the hands of thieves and his own whereabouts unknown.

Roden's cattle (one source says horses) were safely ensconced on Buck Island for the winter, and there was a simple wooden cabin that he had built in his youth—not much more than a shack really—where he or someone else could stay for short periods of time to tend to the cattle and keep them safe from rustlers.

On Christmas Eve 1864, Ben Roden's thirty-four-year-old son, Portland; his forty-year-old nephew, Sergeant James Roden of Company G, Forty-eighth Alabama Infantry, who had been captured at Vicksburg, Mississippi, and paroled; and James's son, nineteen-year-old Private Felix Roden of Company G, Fourth Alabama Cavalry, hid out at Buck Island when they heard that the notorious Union marauder Ben Harris was near. Along with the Rodens was a Confederate soldier named Charles L. Hardcastle of Company C, Fiftieth Alabama Infantry Regiment, who happened to be home on leave. He had enlisted in 1862 in the Paint Rock Rifles. The three Confederates knew that they risked torture, and perhaps death, if Ben Harris and his henchmen were to find them.

Ben Harris, who grew up near Paint Rock, was about thirty years old in 1864. He had been an overseer in Louisiana, and had joined the U.S. Cavalry Regiment in August 1862, but was back in Alabama within two years. He was no stranger to the people of Madison and Marshall Counties, however. Harris was a brutal and cruel man, and he wore a Union coat as he led scouts for the Union army on missions to ferret out those who were known to harbor soldiers or sympathize with the Confederate cause. Harris burned their homes and their crops, stole their livestock and killed them in cold blood. He enjoyed inflicting cruelty, even on his own people. With members of the Union army to back him up, it was futile for anyone to resist. Harris was not *officially* a member of the Union army; he was paid by the day. Those who rode with him may or may not have been sanctioned by the Union army—historians debate this today. They were outfitted and armed by the Union army, although the cost of their gear was probably deducted from their pay. At any rate, Ben Harris took advantage of his Union coat to settle scores and line his pockets as he saw fit.

On December 26, the four men were joined at the Buck Island cabin by patriarch Benjamin Roden, who had already lost his son Andrew the previous year when he was one of the five thousand Americans killed at the Battle of Salem Church, Virginia. The five men shivered in the cold darkness as the fire died down. They pulled their blankets closer and finally drifted off to sleep. At about 2:00 a.m., they were jolted awake by someone pounding on the door. They were ordered to surrender by none other than Ben Harris and twenty-five or so Union cavalrymen. Harris demanded that they raise the sunken ferry and take the cattle belonging to Ben Roden back across the river. Ben Roden, who had known Harris and his family for years, spoke quietly to him, asking that their lives be spared. Harris promised he would not kill them if they complied. But when they finished with the cattle, Harris lined them up and informed them that they were about to die. They were allowed a few minutes to say their prayers, and if they had any valuables to be taken back to their loved ones, he promised to deliver them. Portland Roden emptied his pockets and handed over some things for Harris to deliver to his wife and three young daughters. It was one more promise that Harris had no intention of keeping.

They prayed solemnly and then faced their executioners. The Roden men stood shoulder to shoulder. One by one they were shot, but this wasn't enough to satisfy Harris's cruelty. They were shot again as they lay on the ground, some as many as four times. Charles Hardcastle, who stood at the end of the line, flinched and turned sideways just as the bullet hit him. He fell to the ground but was not dead. The bullet went through his side and lodged in his shoulder. He lay perfectly still on the ground, and for reasons unknown, he was not shot a second time. Someone leaned over to take his pulse but did not find one. Hardcastle, along with the bodies of the four Roden men, were dragged to the river and thrown in.

When Hardcastle hit the cold water, he gasped involuntarily. In the still and murky darkness, his struggle was heard by his would-be murderers. "Stick your saber into his damned body!" someone shouted. The soldiers chopped at the water with their swords. "Knock his brains out with a fence rail!" As luck would have it, the current was swift, and Hardcastle was just out of reach. Two shots were fired as he found a piece of driftwood to hide beneath, with just his nose above water. The soldiers watched for a few minutes, waiting for Hardcastle to resurface. In the meantime, the bodies of the four slain Roden men were carried away by the frigid waters of the Tennessee. Charles Hardcastle would not die at the hands of Ben Harris and his blue-coated marauders. He made his way to shore and collapsed. Sometime later, he gathered enough strength to get up and make his way to the home of his brother-in-law, J.H. Stearns.

Ben Harris's thirst for blood was not yet satisfied. According to another source, Harris and his men went on to the home of Madison Ritchie and hauled him out of bed, made him walk in front of them for several miles, forced him into the Paint Rock River and shot him seven times in the back. On another occasion, Harris found an overseer who had taken the oath of allegiance to the United States but made the fatal mistake of helping a plantation owner drive his stock across the river. For "aiding the Confederacy," the overseer was strung up, and a note was nailed to the tree from which his body swung to and fro, promising death to anyone who dared to cut him down. On yet another occasion, it was reported that Harris robbed a man of several thousand dollars and then told him that he had ten minutes to cross the Tennessee River. If he returned, Harris promised the man that he would hang him until buzzards pecked his eyes out.

The war finally ended, but life would not return to normal for the families of more than 600,000 men. Burned-out homes were rebuilt or abandoned forever. Many started over and many more waited to die, but for most of the country, confusion was all around. Where and how would they fit into the world upended by war? Some would be called upon to account for their sins, but not everyone.

Ben Harris did not meet the cruel and painful end he enjoyed inflicting on others. He died in Madison County near the end of the war and was buried with other dead Union soldiers at Maple Hill Cemetery in Huntsville. When the Union soldiers' bodies were removed and taken to the National Cemetery in Chattanooga for reinterment, Harris's remains were taken too. His headstone reads, "Capt. Benjamin Harris, 13th Indiana Cavalry." His widow, Caroline Vann Harris, applied for a pension on her husband's service but was denied. Later, she took a pair of sharpened scissors and, in the front of her home, slashed her own throat.

Charles Hardcastle, the only survivor of the Buck Island Massacre, moved in with his son in Colbert County, Alabama, sometime before 1910.

The Roden family of Jackson County hosts a family reunion every year. Members make the pilgrimage from all over the United States and clean

The grave of James Roden. *Photograph by Robert Reeves.*

The grave of Felix Roden. *Photograph by Robert Reeves.*

The grave of Portland Roden. *Photograph by Robert Reeves.*

The grave of Benjamin Roden. *Photograph by Robert Reeves.*

the family cemetery where the four Roden men met their tragic deaths in December 1864. The matching headstones of Portland and his father, Benjamin, are inscribed with the date of December 26, 1864. Not all sources, including the story dictated by Charles Hardcastle, agree with this date of death. Weeping willows carved into their stones are the symbols of sorrow and bereavement. There are several family members with government-issued Confederate headstones installed in February 1997, including the two over the graves of Felix and his father, James Roden, with the year of their deaths given as 1863. But the story does not end there. Farther down the cemetery is the headstone of Andrew P. Roden, son of Benjamin Roden, who died in 1863 at Salem Church, Virginia, from a bullet through his head. Next to him lies the body of his wife, Charlotte, whose nearly illegible headstone indicates that she died in 1907. Rumors say that Charlotte turned in her father-in-law, brother-in-law and cousins to Ben Harris because she was bitter at having lost her husband but more perhaps because she wasn't friendly with her husband's relatives. Rumor also has it that she never expected they would die at the hands of Ben Harris.

COLDBLOODED MURDER
THE DEATH OF DR. JACK WILSON

On May 22, 1992, fifty-five-year-old Dr. Jack Wilson, a popular Huntsville ophthalmologist, left his office on Whitesport Circle and made his way up Garth Mountain to his two-story home on the Boulder Circle cul-de-sac. The high-end homes in that southeast neighborhood were well maintained and beautifully landscaped. Dr. Wilson's brick home was, in comparison to those around it, rather average—certainly not ostentatious. There were no particularly outstanding features. It sat on a desirable wooded lot, however, and the neighborhood of professionals was quiet. Dr. Wilson intended to finish packing for a trip he was taking with his wife, Betty, to Santa Fe. They planned to spend a week sightseeing and enjoying good Mexican food in the high desert of New Mexico.

When he arrived at his home, Dr. Wilson changed his clothes, puttered around a little and then decided to stake a campaign sign in his front yard for their friend Tim Morgan, who was in the race for Madison County district attorney. Dr. Wilson found a metal baseball bat, which he used to pound the sign into the ground. When he had finished, he walked back inside the house, carrying the bat with him.

At 9:30 p.m., a police dispatcher received a call from Dr. Wilson's neighbor, summoning police and an ambulance to 2700 Boulder Circle. Officer Jim Donegan was the first to arrive at the home. The dispatcher informed him that there was a possible robbery in progress, and he approached the home cautiously. A light was on in the garage and the front door was ajar. He stepped inside with his pistol in his hand. He glanced quickly into the rooms on the first floor. As he made his way up the stairs, Donegan saw a man lying

The home where Dr. Jack Wilson was murdered has been modified since his 1992 death. *Photograph by Robert Reeves.*

on his back in a bloody mess on the upstairs landing. The man was wearing khaki slacks, a polo shirt and socks, but no shoes. He did not move. Not knowing if the attacker was still in the house, Donegan backed down the stairs and called for more police, as well as paramedics. A thorough search revealed that no one else was in the house and confirmed what he already suspected: Dr. Jack Wilson was dead.

An autopsy revealed gruesome details of the doctor's final moments. He had been hit nine times with the baseball bat. Six of the blows fractured his skull, and his shoulder blade had been broken by another blow. Defensive wounds were present, too. Both forearms bore broken bones, and there were three fractures in his hands. He had also been stabbed twice. According to the autopsy results, he was already near death at the time he was stabbed. In addition, a bone in his neck had been broken, indicating strangulation.

Jack's wife of fourteen years, Betty, discovered her husband's body. She had arrived home after a day of shopping, followed by an Alcoholics Anonymous meeting. She dropped her shopping bags and her purse as soon as she saw her husband's lifeless body and ran from the house to a neighbor's. She was, understandably, hysterical and was not much help to police trying to investigate the murder scene.

Betty told police that she thought her husband must have surprised a burglar. Dr. Wilson's wallet was lying by his body. His cash was gone, but there were several credit cards still inside. Something else seemed unusual. Valuables were all accounted for, no drawers had been ransacked, Mrs. Wilson's jewelry was where she had left it and there were several guns, popular among thieves because they were easy to sell, in plain sight and untouched. Yet a box that had contained a pistol, hidden in Mrs. Wilson's bedroom, was found empty. Stranger still, the phone line in Dr. Wilson's bedroom had been cut.

Dr. Jack Wilson was well known in the Huntsville community and very well liked, even by those who did not understand his quirky nature. When a patient could not pay his bill, Dr. Wilson might say that he would forgive it in return for homemade oatmeal cookies with raisins or set up a hundred-year payment plan, knowing that he would probably not see a dime. He was generous that way, yet frugal with his own money. Jack was a native of Chicago, had served during the Vietnam War and loved the military enough to want to make it a career, but when he was diagnosed with Crohn's disease, he was discharged from the military.

Jack and his first wife, Julia, moved to Huntsville with their three children in July 1968. His business took off, but his marriage did not. In the mid-1970s, he and Julia were divorced. Still, he kept his strange sense of humor and was known for his peculiarities. He set up elaborate practical jokes and put an ad in the newspaper announcing that his office would be closed for the Annual Eye Exam of Elvis Presley. Although his strange brand of humor didn't always find an appreciative audience, no one denied that he was an outstanding doctor and cared for his patients.

And then there was his second wife, Betty. Betty was born on July 14, 1945, raised in nearby Gadsden and had a twin sister, Peggy. They were not identical; in fact, they were very different, yet like most twins, they were cosmically close. They both married shortly after high school and then divorced. Betty had three boys, but when the youngest was only ten months old, she packed up her belongings, left the boys with their father and moved to Huntsville to pursue a nursing career. She was known as quite a party girl to the residents of her Huntsville apartment complex, as well as at the hospital where she worked. She met Jack Wilson and turned on the charm. Her friends knew that she was after a doctor, and before long, they were married.

After Dr. Wilson's surgery in 1982 to attach an ostomy bag, Betty sent him to a separate bedroom. She began to bring one-night stands to their home for sex—with her husband's blessing, according to Betty. And what did he get in return? He once commented that all that money was good for was getting a pretty wife. He drove used cars; she drove a new Mercedes, and her back-up car was a BMW. He reused office envelopes, while she wore an $8,000 Rolex. She had plastic surgery and her makeup was tattooed on. It was Jack's job to make more money than she could spend, and her job was to spend more than he could make. Her spending habits annoyed him considerably, but her caustic verbal abuse toward him made him bite his tongue most of the time.

While investigators were busy looking into clues relating to Dr. Wilson's gruesome murder, police received an odd call from detectives in Shelby County. A woman there had met a man who claimed that he would be paid $5,000 to kill the husband of a twin in Huntsville. And the murder victim was a doctor. As preposterous as the story sounded, it seemed more than a little coincidental. Detectives checked to see if Betty *might* have a twin sister, and suddenly it appeared that the case had solved itself.

James White was picked up in Vincent, Alabama, four days after Dr. Wilson's death. He was a drug addict, had a felony record and psychiatric problems and his work history was sketchy at best. White admitted that he knew Betty Wilson's twin sister Peggy Lowe because he had done carpentry work in her classroom and then at her home. He was supposed to do some work for Peggy's sister, Betty, in Huntsville. He was in love with Peggy; he said he'd had an affair with her and would do anything she asked.

White was questioned by Huntsville investigators and brought to Huntsville, where he confessed to the murder in exchange for leniency. Even though he knew details of the crime, he lacked credibility. His version of the murder changed with every telling, and no one knew what to believe.

In the meantime, Peggy Lowe and Betty Wilson were staying in the Huntsville home of their older sister while police continued their investigation. Their brother-in-law heard that James White had been arrested for murder and rushed to knock on the door to the guest room to tell them the great news. Their reaction was not at all what he expected. It seemed odd to him that they didn't make any comment whatsoever.

In spite of James White's wobbly and inconsistent confession, parts of it made sense. White had driven to Huntsville once before to commit the murder, but when he arrived, he discovered that Betty's son was at the house. He turned around and went back to Vincent. Betty insisted, through Peggy, that the murder be completed before their trip to Santa Fe, but he told Peggy that he couldn't do it because he didn't have a weapon.

On Wednesday, May 20, Peggy called White to tell him that they had the "tool for the job." The two sisters met him in a remote location to give him a .38 Smith & Wesson revolver. When police asked him later why he didn't use the weapon, his answer was simple: he disliked guns ever since his stint in Vietnam.

White told police that he had been advanced $2,500 for the murder. He paid some bills, caught up somewhat on his child support and frittered away the rest. As the day of the murder grew near, he needed more money for expenses, so Betty told him to go to the front desk at Guntersville State Lodge, where she was attending a retreat sponsored by Alcoholics Anonymous. She had put $200 into a library book entitled *The Sleeping Beauty and the Firebird* checked out of the Huntsville-Madison County Library and left it for him.

On May 22, the day of the murder, Betty left a paper bag with more money in it at a fast-food restaurant in the Parkway City Mall. She then gave White a ride to her house, unlocked the door and let him inside to wait for Jack Wilson. Betty left the house and waited. They had agreed ahead of time that she would call her house, and if White had finished the job, he would pick up the phone and hang it up. She called every few minutes, while White waited for Jack to come home. James White nearly lost his nerve and left. Dr. Wilson came home later than expected because he was getting caught up at the office before his trip out of town. While going up the stairs, he was confronted by his killer. They struggled, and Dr. Wilson put up quite a fight, but he was a small, frail man and in the end his struggle was not enough.

Betty called again, and this time White picked up the phone. She rushed home and picked up White. He crouched down in the seat so that no one would see him. In her haste to take White back to his truck, Betty caused a neighbor to swerve her car to avoid a collision. White drove back to Vincent, Alabama, and like most criminals who get caught for committing crimes, he couldn't keep his mouth shut. This proved to be his undoing because there was nothing to link any of the three to the crime scene besides his admission of guilt.

On Tuesday, May 26, Jack Wilson's funeral was held. Peggy Lowe was supposed to return to Vincent that day and leave the final $2,500 for White in a box in her garage, but before that could happen, Shelby County authorities picked him up for questioning. Within a few days, Betty took $85,000 out of the joint account she had with Jack and set up her own account—just in case.

Peggy and Betty were picked up by police and charged with murder. Huntsville was stunned. Those who knew Betty Wilson, however, were not. As much as people loved her husband, they disliked Betty. She was abrasive and demanding. She slept around and despised her husband. And yet she mentored new members of Alcoholics Anonymous with kindness and care.

Huntsville attorney Charlie Hooper headed a team of attorneys hired to defend Betty. Marc Sandlin would defend her sister Peggy. Peggy was released on $150,000 bond, but Betty was denied bail. Jack's three sons took legal action to prevent Betty from receiving her inheritance until after her trial and, of course, only if she received an acquittal. Furthermore, she was required to restore the cash she had removed from their joint bank account. It was decided that the sisters would be tried separately, and due to intense media coverage, Judge Thomas Younger granted a change in venue.

On February 23, 1993, Betty Wilson's trial began at the courthouse on Greensboro Avenue in Tuscaloosa, Alabama. The state attorney general assigned Limestone County district attorney Jimmy Fry to prosecute the case. It seemed that the entire case hinged on the effectiveness of James White to convince the jury of Betty's role, but because his story waffled so much, it would be difficult. Fortunately, White's nine months in jail forced him to dry out, and perhaps his thinking was a little clearer.

Betty's team of defense lawyers evolved and grew. The legendary Georgia attorney Bobby Lee Cook was hired; he was reputed to be one of the best criminal attorneys in the United States. Joseph Colquitt and Jack Drake of Tuscaloosa joined the team as well. Madison County judge Thomas Younger, who granted the change of venue, presided over the trial.

Prosecutor Jimmy Fry carefully questioned James White to establish his credibility as a witness, but defense attorney Bobby Lee Cook went on the offensive to discredit White's testimony. He asked White about the change of clothing found under a rock at the Wilson residence some time after the murder. White admitted that the bag contained the clothing he had worn to commit the murder. He also said that it had been put there later, implying that it was done by Betty or Peggy. A knife was found with the clothing, but water had seeped into the plastic grocery bag and compromised everything inside. Even though White ran fast and loose with the truth, he remained relatively calm and unshaken on the stand under the grueling questioning by defense attorney Bobby Lee Cook. Prosecutors rebounded when they brought in a number of witnesses to corroborate White's testimony and coincide with the timeline leading up to the murder. Others were brought in to describe how Betty frequently spoke to her husband condescendingly. In her defense, Betty's son testified, as did her sister Peggy and Peggy's husband. Finally, the testimony was over.

On March 2, 1993, the jury began to deliberate on Betty Wilson's fate. After eleven hours, the jury returned a verdict of guilty. She was sentenced to life in prison without parole.

Six months later, Peggy Lowe was tried for the same crime in Montgomery before another judge from Madison County, Judge William Page. Attorney General Don Valeska prosecuted Peggy. She was defended by David C. Johnson of Birmingham and Herman "Buck" Watson of Huntsville. While the spectators in Betty's trial were predominantly against her, most of the people at Peggy's trial were there to support her. People from her church were there to pray for her and to show the jury that she was a good Christian woman. Nine days after the trial began, and less than two and a half hours after the case went to the jury, the jury returned with an acquittal.

In the end, everyone had an opinion about Betty's guilt. Nearly everyone believed that one sister could not be innocent and the other guilty; either one of them was wrongly convicted or the other was wrongly acquitted. But there are many truths that may have factored into the jury's decision. Betty stood to gain most of Jack's $6 million estate. Her behavior—having her hairdresser brought from Huntsville to fix her hair for her appearance in court and her blatant public distaste and humiliation for her husband, as well as her many sexual liaisons—didn't garner much public sympathy.

Most people in Huntsville assume that Betty's sentence was just and that her sister Peggy got away with murder. There are still unanswered questions that will never be addressed. James White, while admitting that he hit Dr. Wilson with a baseball bat, denied stabbing him with a knife. It was suggested that Betty came into the house and found her husband still alive, then finished him off with a knife. James White claimed that he had a fling with Peggy Lowe and even described her underwear. He also said that the plan was to take Peggy's husband out on the lake in a boat and stage an accident in which he would drown. Not long after Peggy's acquittal, she and her husband quietly divorced.

James Dennison White, born March 4, 1951, is incarcerated in the Western Alabama town of Hamilton. Prisoner #174225 lives in the Hamilton Aged and Infirmed facility. He was sentenced to life in prison with the possibility of parole; however, no parole date is listed.

Betty Wilson, prisoner #171316, lives at Tutwiler State Prison. Her appeals have been exhausted, and the family home where Dr. Jack Wilson died sold only days after it was put on the market. Huntsville resident Bill

Campbell fell in love with Betty, and they were married at Tutwiler Prison on May 1, 2006.

Perhaps no contemporary Huntsville murder has elicited more speculation and discussion than that of Dr. Jack Wilson. The story has all the makings of a salacious novel, along with a who's who of well-known local names. Betty has always claimed that she was convicted not because she hired someone to kill her husband, but because it was revealed during her trial that she had an affair with a black man. In other words, her assertion is that the bigotry of the jury was greater than the evidence against her. Her accusation is an insult to the intelligence of the jury that found her guilty of murder, as well as the people of Alabama.

THE SOUTHWEST MOLESTER

In the early morning hours of November 27, 1978, a twenty-year-old woman living on McVay Street in Huntsville woke up to see a shadowy figure standing in the doorway of her darkened bedroom. She screamed. A masked man quickly put his hand over her mouth and a knife to her throat. "Shut up!" he snarled. "I need money!"

The young woman told him she had five dollars in her purse. The intruder, who had cut her telephone line, tied her hands behind her back with a length of cord and gagged her, securing the gag with duct tape. He ordered her to turn and face the wall. After going through her dresser drawers, he asked her if she was married or if she had any nude pictures of herself. He forced her to stand up and began to assault her sexually with his hand. She began to choke, and the gag was nearly out of her mouth when he ordered her back onto the bed. He tied one leg to the bed and then cut off her panties and shirt with his knife. He began to rape her with something sharp and painful, and when she flinched, he poked her with the tip of his knife. As the sexual assault intensified, he told her he had been castrated in an insane asylum. He then assaulted her sexually with a whiskey bottle and a tube of mascara. When he was satisfied that he had tortured her enough, he left. The terrified young woman struggled until she had freed herself from the cord and gag. Quickly, she put on clothing, climbed out her bedroom window and ran to a neighbor's house to call the police.

On December 14, 1978, a seventeen-year-old girl who lived on Troy Swasey Boulevard said goodbye to her boyfriend as he left for work. She returned to the kitchen to prepare a cup of hot tea. She heard the door open and assumed that her boyfriend had returned for something or that her brother was coming home early from work. But it was neither one. A stranger lunged at her and held a weapon against her stomach. Ominously, he locked the door behind him, forced her into the bedroom and made her sit on a chair. He turned up the radio, stuffed a hamburger bun in her mouth and taped it in place with electrical tape. The masked stranger put her facedown on the bed, tied her hands behind her back and, as he had the victim before, raped her with an inanimate object. He sliced the bottoms of her feet, punched, beat and whipped her between her legs and then picked her up off the bed and dropped her face first onto the floor. He continued to beat her.

The intruder went through dresser drawers looking for cash. He returned her to the bed and forced her legs apart until she screamed from the pain. He punched her in the stomach and then punched her again. He tied her ankles to the bed and began to torture her more, whipping and cutting her. As she screamed in pain, he put a pillow over her face to suffocate her. She fought him, and he tried to put tape over her nose so she couldn't breathe.

Suddenly, the intruder was startled by the sound of the victim's brother unlocking the front door and entering the apartment. He escaped through the window. The young woman's brother found her, untied her and told her to go into the bathroom, lock the door and wait. Her brother went out the same window after the intruder. But it was too late—the assailant was long gone.

In May 1978, a man who would become known as the Southwest Molester began to terrorize women by breaking into their homes, tying them up and sexually torturing them. Because the intensity of his torture began to escalate with each new victim, police feared that he might soon turn to murder. Police assigned to the task force were losing sleep over the case, and one was beginning to get paranoid that the attacker was playing a cat-and-mouse game with him personally.

Two women were attacked in May 1978, two in November and two more in December. Another attempt was made on a woman in January 1979, and it was believed that additional attempts were interrupted. Jim Hall, eight years old at the time, was climbing the apple tree in his yard when he noticed cigarette butts in the nearby alley off Atlantic Street. The Southwest Molester had entered his family home the night before, thinking that Jim's mother was alone with the children. Her husband got out of bed and ran him off. The police were called, and it was determined that the intruder was indeed the molester. Cigarette butts at the scene indicated that he had watched the family for some time, smoking, while he waited for the right moment to attack.

The women, all of whom were white, ranged in age from seventeen to twenty-five and lived in the southwest part of Huntsville. Over 150 suspects were questioned and cleared in the first ten months of the investigation. Police Chief Gene Sweeton assured the people of Huntsville that the capture of the Southwest Molester was his number one priority. As fear began to grow and spread, the number of women taking self-defense classes increased dramatically. The sale of guns went up as well, and the attacks were a topic of conversation everywhere. Women especially looked over their shoulders or asked someone to walk with them to their cars and front doors, but still there were enough who didn't take these precautions. A reward of $10,000 was offered for evidence leading to the molester's conviction. Alabama governor Fob James signed a law into effect making sexual abuse a felony if the attacker entered the victim's home. Still, the attacks continued.

As careful as he was not to leave fingerprints or be seen by anyone, the Southwest Molester finally made a mistake. In September 1979, he raped a twenty-three-year-old woman on Miller Lane in the Big Cove community. He parked his car off the road, and this gave police the break they had been looking for. The dirt was soft, and the car's tires left visible impressions. With a vague description of the car from an eyewitness and a plaster-cast imprint made from the tire tracks in the dirt, police canvassed tire stores and learned everything they could about the characteristics of tire treads. The tracks identified the tires as one of five styles found on Japanese cars. The tread width and distance between the tires identified the car as a Subaru. The depth of the tread told investigators approximately how old the tires were. It was an incredible long shot, but with that information, police visited dealerships in Huntsville, and their investigation led them to Universal Volkswagen-Subaru on North Memorial Parkway. A man named John Paul Dejnozka had bought a 1979 two-door blue Subaru coupe in July 1979.

At a 6:00 a.m. press conference on Saturday, September 22, 1979, Deputy Chief of Police Bobby Smith announced that an arrest had been made the evening before. The man known as the Southwest Molester was in custody. John Paul Dejnozka, age thirty-five, was arrested on the afternoon of September 21, 1979, as he drove from work in his blue Subaru. The entire molester squad, which had worked tirelessly on the case, was present during the arrest to make sure that the suspect could not escape. District Attorney Fred Simpson stated, "I hope people realize they have an outstanding police department. Through hard work they apprehended this man. Hopefully prosecution will do its job now and see this man to the penitentiary."

The police, who had been under intense pressure to catch the molester, felt the release of an enormous burden. Detectives singled out for their dedication to the case were Charles Norment, Ron Curlee, Wayne Sharp, Dick Yearick and Jim Stewart.

Everyone wanted to know more about the man who had become known as the Southwest Molester. He was unassuming, quiet and somewhat of a loner. His personality, according to those who met him, was low key, almost boring. Dejnozka was employed as a quality control analyst for Office Systems of America at 4717 University Drive, and he had been promoted three times. In addition, he was an Amway salesman. Now that he had been caught, all eyes were focused on the system of justice that would punish him for his crimes.

Bonds totaling $2.16 million were set by Judge S.A. "Bud" Watson. Richard Kempaner and Bruce Williams were appointed to defend Dejnozka. He now faced forty-one charges, which included attacks on eighteen female victims, including a woman in Athens. District Attorney Fred Simpson and Assistant District Attorney Charles Hooper would prosecute.

As investigators and prosecutors prepared the case against John Paul Dejnozka, they uncovered interesting details of his life before he moved to Huntsville. He was born in New Jersey and had been convicted of aggravated kidnapping, rape and burglary in Alton, Illinois, in 1974. He was sentenced to serve twelve years in prison. In February 1977, after only three years, he was paroled and came to Huntsville, where his brother lived. Dejnozka lived on Barclay Avenue in Southwest Huntsville and took a job as a computer specialist. Dejnozka was required to report to a parole officer and did so until April 5, 1979, when he was discharged from parole from his rape conviction in Illinois. Ironically, by this time Dejnozka had already been terrorizing Huntsville women for the better part of a year.

In July 1978, Dejnozka moved to Haystack Apartments on Sparkman Drive. The complex, which appealed especially to young singles, was known for the many social activities held for its residents. Dejnozka, who lived in apartment 39A, served on several social committees within the complex so he could get to know his Haystack neighbors better. He went to Monday night football events and even won first prize at the annual Halloween party. When asked about his background, he said he had "worked" in a prison before coming to Huntsville. He even started attending a local church.

Between the hours of 2:00 and 4:00 a.m., Dejnozka would get restless and get in his car, drive somewhere and walk. He claimed that he went no place in particular, he just needed to get out and clear his mind. But police knew that he was a dangerous and devious predator and he was not looking to clear his mind; rather, he was stalking his prey. He watched for clues that women were at home without an adult male present. It could be that too many outside lights were on or perhaps a car was parked on the edge of a driveway to leave room for another car. He usually entered the home through an open window or unlocked door, covered his face with a T-shirt and sometimes took a weapon from inside the house or carried one with him. His weapon of choice was a knife, but he once used the leg from a table and even a sharp nail. He would gag his victim and wrap tape around her mouth. He would pull a switch off of a tree and hit her with it repeatedly. He once used a car antenna to beat a victim. The victims were consistent in their descriptions of the methods he used to torture them. One woman had a bandage over her breast from recent surgery. She asked him not to cause any permanent damage. He later said, "I didn't want to cause anybody any permanent injury and I ran from that one." In fact, he did just the opposite, breaking the wound open, causing her to bleed and necessitating a trip to the hospital. One woman made him angry because she smelled bad and was on welfare. He disapproved and attacked her.

He said in his confession to Detective Wayne Sharp and Sheriff's Investigator Jim Stewart that his attacks were based on anger, not on sexual fantasies. He blamed pressure at work for causing him to commit the crimes, and in times when there was a lull in the attacks, he said it was because his workload had lightened up. Through media reports, he knew when and where stakeouts were set up and avoided those areas. One night, he was nearly caught by police when he entered an apartment off Patton Road.

Dejnozka's biggest regret, he admitted, was that he had been caught at a time when he was about to achieve financial independence through his job and by selling Amway products. He regretted that he had been caught now that he was in a relationship that he felt had potential. It seemed that the only regret he didn't have was for what he did to his victims.

A special grand jury was convened. Dejnozka was kept isolated in a four-foot by six-foot cell. The charges against him stacked up. There were twenty-eight indictments that contained forty-one counts brought against him: twelve counts of first-degree burglary, two counts of rape, one count of second-degree burglary, twelve counts of flogging, thirteen counts of assault with intent to maim and one count of sexual abuse. Limestone County also issued a warrant for first-degree burglary and the assault of an Athens woman. Dejnozka's defense attorneys requested a change of venue, asking that the trial be moved to Birmingham because of intense publicity.

On November 6, Judge Watson denied the request for a change of venue. He also ordered that a mental test on Dejnozka be conducted by someone from the Huntsville-Madison County Mental Health Center.

Test results revealed that Dejnozka scored in the upper 2.2 percent of the population in terms of intelligence. There was no evidence that his thinking was impaired, that he had an illness such as schizophrenia or that he was manic-depressive. He was diagnosed as having an antisocial personality and as being a sadistic sexual deviant. He fantasized about torture, rape and inflicting mental pain. He had no guilt, was prone to frustration and could not be loyal to any individual or group of people. He had no social values, and he was selfish, impulsive and resistant to learning from punishment or his mistakes. In fact, he blamed others for his crimes. The examiner also recommended that Dejnozka was suitable to stand trial, was responsible for his actions and that, if convicted, he should be held accountable for the crimes he had committed.

As it turned out, Dejnozka had known one of his victims superficially before he attacked her. She did not recognize his voice during the attack and did not realize, in the months afterward, that the man she was beginning to know well through their involvement in Amway sales was the man who had caused her so much pain. He said during his confession that of all his attacks, perhaps this was the one he was most sorrowful about. As he got to know her and her husband, he realized what "fine Christian people" they were.

On March 27, 1980, Dejnozka was led before Judge Watson in the Madison County Courthouse with his attorneys. He entered a plea of not guilty.

Defense attorney Richard Kempaner was quoted in the newspaper as saying, "[Dejnozka is] a nice guy, intelligent, well-rounded. I just *like* the guy." Kempaner went on to say that anyone who would try to hurt Dejnozka just didn't know him. Yet those who spent time interrogating him had a different story to tell. His demeanor was cold, unemotional and unremorseful. He downplayed his responsibilities for the attacks and complained that if he had someone to talk to about his troubles, he wouldn't have had to take out his frustrations the way he did.

Security was tight for the trial, which began on Monday, March 31, 1980, and the courtroom was filled with, among others, many of his victims. Everyone who entered the courtroom was frisked for concealed weapons. Of the prospective jurors who were questioned, two men said that they could not judge him fairly, and one woman worked with one of his victims. A jury of nine men and three women was struck. District Attorney Fred Simpson told the jury that no one would be excused because he or she had heard about the case.

Dejnozka was tried, first, for the attack on the woman who lived on Miller Lane in the Big Cove community. He took the witness stand, outside of the jury's presence, and admitted that he had given a confession to police, only because he believed that he would receive psychiatric treatment at a hospital rather than spend time in prison. Despite the objection of the defense attorneys, his confession was read to the jury. The trial, which had been much anticipated all over Huntsville, was over the next day. After deliberating for thirty minutes, the jury found Dejnozka guilty. He was sentenced to 150 years in prison, and by four o'clock that afternoon he was on his way to Kilby Correctional Institute near Montgomery. Unfortunately, even with a 150-year sentence, he could be out of prison in 5 years and 3 months for good behavior.

District Attorney Fred Simpson announced that a letter-writing campaign would be launched to demand that the legislature change the Good Time law, which would make Dejnozka eligible to get out of prison for good behavior. Over three thousand letters were received.

On October 28, 1980, Dejnozka was back in Huntsville for yet another trial. Defense attorney Richard Kempaner was released from the case because he was running for the office of district attorney. The trial was over shortly after noon, and Judge Watson added another 150 years onto Dejnozka's previous sentence. Before it was all over, he was sentenced to 830 years in prison.

Still, Dejnozka was allowed to apply for parole. At his March 2004 parole hearing, his first victim arrived with a petition signed by 2,054 people opposing his parole. "Dejnozka has served just over twenty-four years of his sentence," she said. "I've already served twenty-six years. There's no parole for me." In five minutes, his parole was denied.

When Dejnozka was interviewed in 1980, he defended himself by saying, "How can they condemn what they don't know about...There was no way even I could have foreseen any of what has happened to me." When asked what he had to say about his victims, he replied, "In the general sense, I feel sorry for anybody that is in pain, whether physical or emotional." But everyone doubted his sincerity.

Dejnozka's brother was horrified to learn that his own flesh and blood had committed the crimes against the people of Huntsville. He flew to their mother's home to break the news to her personally. He encouraged his brother to confess, if he was indeed guilty of the crimes. After his brother's conviction, he broke off contact with him. He died recently of cancer.

Alabama inmate records indicate that John Paul Dejnozka, born November 9, 1943, is now incarcerated at Holman Correctional Facility. His release date is listed as September 10, 2391. He has something to look forward to.

UNDER THE POND

David and Debbie Stewart were going through a rough patch in their marriage. Six months after the birth of her third child, Debbie still suffered from the effects of postpartum depression, also known as "baby blues." On top of the stress of caring for three children, one from her first marriage, money was scarce. David hoped they would work things out and climb out of their financial rut. But after an argument one hot July night in 1984, Debbie announced that she was leaving David. Furthermore, she was taking the children with her, far away from Decatur, Alabama.

Debbie Stewart was never seen again.

Debbie was an attractive woman. At age thirty-six, she stood five feet, six inches tall and weighed 130 pounds. She had auburn hair and blue-green eyes. She was a registered nurse but quit work to stay at home with her young children. She had been left a widowed mother when her first husband, a U.S. soldier, was murdered in Korea. But she found happiness again when she married David Stewart, and soon two more children were added to the family.

David Stewart, born in 1952, was a good-looking and youthful thirty-two-year-old. Those who knew him described him as soft-spoken, mild-mannered, easygoing and quiet. He had a job, but his salary wasn't quite enough to cover the growing family's expenses.

On the morning of July 11, Debbie's father expected her to show up and drive him to work. Instead, it was David who came and explained, to her father's apparent satisfaction, that he would drive him. Over the next few weeks, however, Debbie's family became concerned that they had not heard from her. The Stewarts' neighbor was concerned as well. David told one neighbor that he was angry because Debbie had called from New Orleans to inform him she was not coming home, leaving him alone to care for their children. After three weeks without any news, Debbie Stewart's sister convinced David that it was time to file a missing person's report. To appease his in-laws, David filed the report. In case she decided to return to take the children away from him, David also filed a petition to have Debbie involuntarily committed to a state mental facility.

Everyone in the family said that Debbie would never simply walk away from her children, no matter what. A neighbor told police that it didn't make any sense for her to leave home without a car. Furthermore, the neighbor had watched, from her window, as David dug a hole in his backyard, soon after Debbie left, and poured concrete into it—at night.

Three weeks turned into months. The oppressive summer heat faded into fall and then the bitter winter cold settled in. As the months passed, one by one, the anger David felt at having been abandoned by his wife began to dim and blur. But the Stewarts' neighbor, who had spoken to Debbie four times on July 10, 1984, and never again, refused to give up her search for the truth behind her friend's sudden disappearance.

The police were concerned as well. At the beginning of the investigation, they questioned David Stewart, followed up on leads, and asked David for permission to dig in his yard to search for Debbie's body. David refused to allow an excavation, and without his consent or probable cause, all that anyone could do was wait.

Almost any time a husband or wife is murdered or missing, police automatically suspect the spouse first. This is the person who usually takes, and/or gives, the most verbal, physical or emotional abuse. This is the person who usually knows what buttons to push to get a reaction. Most importantly, the spouse is usually the person with the most to gain. Most murders are committed for financial gain, to keep a secret or because of pure, white-hot anger.

The years passed, goldfish swam in the concrete pond that David dug in the darkness one summer night in 1984 and the Stewart children played in the backyard of their Decatur home. David Stewart went to work every day, yet his neighbor continued to watch and wait. She was finally rewarded for her patience.

David Stewart fell behind on his house payments. The bank foreclosed on his property, and in 1987, it was auctioned. It was sold to a couple for $85,000. They began the process of remodeling the house and prepared for their move. The new owners were looking at the home one day when their soon-to-be neighbor, the woman who had repeatedly tried to convince the police that David Stewart had killed his wife, stepped out of her home to have a chat. She told them everything. No, Debbie had not walked out on her husband and children, and no, she was not living a carefree life in New Orleans or anywhere else. She was dead, the neighbor insisted, and buried under the fishpond. At her urging, the new owners called police and gave them permission to dig up their yard.

On August 19, 1987, shortly after noon, police arrived at the home on 2323 Springdale Road. With them were several city workers with jackhammers and shovels. An hour after they began, a heavy black plastic bag was unearthed. Dismembered human remains were found inside. Police pulled up at the Lurleen B. Wallace Developmental Center, where David Stewart worked as a counselor, and astonished co-workers watched as Stewart was handcuffed and taken away. By four o'clock that afternoon, he was formally booked for murder.

The following day, Police Captain Ken Collier announced that William David Stewart had been arrested. Several bags containing dismembered body parts had been recovered from his former home. "I hoped she wouldn't be there," the neighbor said to a newspaper reporter, "but I knew she was."

Everyone with whom David worked walked around in disbelief. Co-worker Beverly Jolly said that those who knew him had felt sorry for him, having to raise his children alone after his wife had abandoned him. Stewart was easy to work with, very nice looking and certainly had no trouble finding women to date. Beverly worked with David, and while she knew the potential risk of dealing with unpredictable patients, she was shaken to find out that the real danger to her safety was one of the people she trusted the most.

Stewart entered a plea of not guilty by reason of insanity. The grand jury impaneled to decide if charges would be brought against him ruled that he would be charged with murder, but his actions did not meet the requirements that constituted a charge of capital murder. A noncapital murder indictment was handed down. Stewart's bail was set at $250,000. He remained in jail while awaiting his trial. His defense attorney, Norman Roby, asked for a change of venue due to the publicity. That request was denied.

One year and one month later, on September 19, 1988, David Stewart walked into the fourth-floor courtroom of the Morgan County Courthouse wearing a coat and tie. His footsteps were short. The dragging chains attached to the shackles on his legs clanked loudly and echoed as he made his way to his chair. The tedious process of questioning potential jurors began. One

David Stewart at the time of his trial.

woman said that she had taught one of the Stewart children, and when asked if she could render a fair and impartial decision, she responded, "Deep down in my heart, I don't know."

A jury, composed of eight women and four men, along with two alternates, was finally struck. Bob Burrell prosecuted the high-profile case of *Alabama v. William David Stewart*. During his opening statement, Burrell painted a picture of the events of July 10, 1984. Stewart had already confessed twice, Burrell told the jury. He wanted the maximum of ninety-nine years in prison for David Stewart. Debbie Stewart's sister sat next to Burrell.

Defense attorney Norman Roby, in his opening statement, portrayed David Stewart as a reasonable man, mild-mannered, easygoing and nice. He went on to say that Stewart was wound tighter than a rubber band and was driven to the breaking point by financial burdens and marital problems. "He snapped," Roby offered, but he did not deserve to spend the rest of his life in prison.

The courtroom was packed; in fact, many people had to stand during the proceedings. Everyone had an opinion about the suggestion that Stewart could be confined to a state mental facility until he was considered cured. On the other hand, he could get as little time as ten years in prison.

Debbie Stewart's sister was among the first witnesses called to testify for the prosecution. She recalled that it took three weeks for her to convince David to file a missing person's report, which he did on July 31, 1984.

Medical examiner Dr. Kenneth Warner of Tuscaloosa recalled the results of the autopsy he performed on the remains of Debbie Stewart. She had a black eye, and two inches of her neck were missing. Because of decomposition, Dr. Warner was not able to rule on an exact cause of death.

Finally, David Stewart took the witness stand in his own defense. Throughout his testimony, he averted his eyes away from the jury. Details of his life with Debbie were brought out through questioning. He and Debbie had met in 1975. She had a five-month-old baby with her deceased first husband. Soon after meeting, they moved in together. Three years later, in 1978, they married. They moved into a house on Springdale Road, and Debbie gave birth to their first child in 1979. Their second child, a daughter, was born in 1984. Debbie had already quit her job as a nurse. At some point in time, they began to remodel their house extensively, including the costly addition of a second story. The financial pressures were taking a toll on their marriage. According to David, Debbie nagged him about his salary and called him "spineless" for not asking for more money at work. He said that she refused to go back to work to help out financially, nor would she agree to file for bankruptcy or move into a less expensive home. On top of that, Debbie had been suffering from postpartum depression since the birth of their daughter.

On July 10, 1984, David came home to find his wife sitting in the dark. While neighbors were at the Stewart home earlier that day, a service representative from the utility company had come to turn off the electricity. Debbie was terribly embarrassed when she was told that the utility check had bounced because of insufficient funds in their bank account. David and Debbie argued. Debbie packed a gym bag and left. Sometime around 10:00 p.m., Debbie returned and informed David that she was going to take the children with her and move to Texas. David was angry. He threw a book at her, hitting her in the head. He picked up a jump rope that one of the children had dropped on the floor and wrapped it around Debbie's neck. He tightened it until her struggling stopped.

Because blood was coming out of her nose and mouth, David took her lifeless body into the master bathroom and put her in the shower. Should he call the police? He thought about his options but decided to hide the crime because he did not want to be taken away from his children, who needed him more now that their mother was gone.

One can only guess what was going on in his mind as he took a utility razor blade and a hacksaw and cut his wife's body into eight pieces. He decided that it would be much more difficult to get rid of a whole body than one in pieces. He wrapped the body parts in newspaper and placed them in plastic bags. (He added lime at some point to kill the smell of decomposition.)

Stewart carried the bags upstairs and placed them in an unfinished bathroom until he could decide what to do with them. He locked the door, checked on his sleeping children and went to bed.

No doubt, he considered many options about what to do with Debbie's body. When his sister-in-law pressured him into filing the missing person's report, he probably knew that police would launch an investigation and search his house. He had to move quickly. He decided to build a fishpond in the backyard, with Debbie's body buried underneath. He hired someone to help him dig a five-foot hole, but when he deemed the hole deep enough, he told the contractor that he would finish it himself. David began the process of transferring the plastic bags from the locked bathroom into the hole, being careful not to do it when anyone was watching. He placed his wife's head closest to the house so it would be close to him and her children. When it was time to pour the cement, he said a prayer over her remains. He drew the curiosity of his suspicious neighbor, however, when he waited until it was dark to do the work.

Stewart installed a liner and landscaped around the pond. He said he went to the fishpond almost daily to pray and talk to his wife, sharing with her the activities of their children. He told his dead wife that he kept the landscaping pretty just for her. "I wanted her close by me and I felt she wanted to be close to her children," Stewart explained when asked why he kept her on the property.

"Why did you kill her?" he was asked.

"Because she was taking my children away from me."

As attorney Robert Tweedy continued to ask questions about the events that brought Stewart to this point, Stewart broke down in tears. He left the witness stand until he could compose himself.

His testimony continued. For three years, Stewart told the same story to police, family and friends. He even had someone in New Orleans call him collect occasionally from different pay phones so that he could present evidence to Debbie's family and to police that she was still alive and well and it was she who had left him. Debbie's brother went to New Orleans to look for her and enlisted the help of the New Orleans police department. Fliers with her picture were put up all over the city.

Within a few months of Debbie's disappearance, Stewart began to date a fifteen-year-old girl.

Occasionally, Debbie's family pressed the police to renew the investigation. Police continued to ask Stewart's permission to dig in the yard, but Stewart refused. His financial troubles continued. After a few years, he stopped making payments on his home, and then the bank began foreclosure proceedings. He and his children moved to a duplex at 824 Johnston Street, and the family home, with the body of Debbie Stewart in the backyard, was sold at auction. When asked what his reaction was when he learned that police had dug up his wife's body on August 19, 1987, Stewart said he felt that police had "interrupted something holy."

Throughout the week of the trial, the courtroom continued to be crowded. At one point, Circuit Judge Rudolph Slate had to stop the trial to confront women lined up on the back wall talking to one another.

Defense Attorney Roby began to explore the manner in which Stewart was questioned after his arrest. He had not been advised of his right to remain silent, the attorney claimed, and furthermore, he was taunted with threats of the electric chair by Officers Jep Tallent and Johnny Bradford, suggesting that Stewart confessed under duress. His arguments changed nothing.

On September 22, 1988, four years after Debbie Stewart was strangled to death, the case was handed over to the jury. After only one hour of deliberation, the jury returned to announce its decision. In spite of the best efforts put forth by Stewart's defense attorneys, the foreman announced that William David Stewart was found guilty of murder. Stewart revealed no emotion as the verdict was read.

On November 15, 1988, Judge Rudolph Slate sentenced Stewart to the maximum of ninety-nine years in prison. The judge explained that the punishment did not fit the heinous crime, but by law he was not allowed to impose a stiffer sentence. "There are no marital pressures to justify what you did," he said.

Judge Slate then ordered Stewart to pay his children $10,000 through the Victims' Compensation Fund. William David Stewart will spend the rest of his life in prison. He is currently incarcerated at Easterling Correctional Facility. No release date is indicated in his record.

The sad story of the death of Debbie Stewart did not end with the conviction of her husband. Several years later, a woman wrote a book of fiction that was eerily similar to the Debbie Stewart murder case. Morgan County circuit judge Richard Hundley ordered that the book not be published. It was his wish that the innocent children of Debbie Stewart be protected from the grisly details of their mother's murder.

DIED IN YOUNG MANHOOD

Governor Thomas Bibb owned one of the most enviable pieces of property in Limestone County. The rich soil, bordering the Tennessee River, was perfect for growing cotton, the crop that made many men wealthy. His plantation home, Belle Manor, was built in 1826 and became the centerpiece of the community that grew up around it. According to legend, when the railroad bisected the community, an official was sent up and down the line to map the small towns and crossroads. When he inquired about the name of the settlement, someone with a very southern accent responded. With an ear perhaps untrained in southern dialect, the official heard the name Belle Manor as "Belle Mina." And so it remains today.

By 1828, Governor Bibb's fifth child, Porter Bibb, lived in the Belle Manor mansion with his wife, the former Mary Pleasants Betts. In this home, they raised their seven children. One, however, met a premature and especially horrible death.

Thomas, born in 1843, was fourteen when he started out for a pleasant day of hunting in the summer of 1858. Details of the event are sketchy but vivid. Not far from his home, Thomas was met by eighteen-year-old Larkin, one of his father's slaves. The *Athens Herald* reported that Larkin summoned Thomas into the woods, telling him he had found a turkey's nest and wanted to show it to him.

When the two were deep into the woods, away from anyone who could be a potential witness, Larkin hit Thomas five or six times in the head and left him for dead when he was called by another slave. About an hour and a half later, Larkin returned to the attack scene and found that Thomas was

The Limestone County mansion built by Governor Thomas Bibb. *Photograph courtesy of the Huntsville-Madison County Public Library.*

still breathing, though probably unconscious. Larkin shot Thomas with his gun, leaving no doubt that the young man was finally dead. He then carried Thomas's body to a pond and sunk it with logs.

An Athens newspaper article reported:

> *It has seldom fallen to our lot to record a more shocking and barbarous murder and one perpetrated under circumstances of more atrocity than the one committed upon the body of Thos. Bibb, a youth about fourteen years old, and son of D.P. Bibb, Esq., near Mooresville in this county on Tuesday week by a negro belonging to Mr. Bibb, named Larkin.*

The July 8, 1858 *Southern Advocate* printed the following story:

> *Horrible Murder—On Tuesday of last week the 29th Inst., Thomas Bibb, a sprightly son of Porter Bibb, Esq., aged about 13 years, living near Mooresville, Alabama, left his father's house to go to a neighbor's on a hunting excursion. He took with him a double barrel shotgun, about three pounds of shot and powder in proportion. His absence for several days, therefore, excited no surprise. But on Friday morning last,*

his dead body was found about a quarter of a mile from his father's house. His skull had been badly broken by a billet of wood found near by, and several small shot holes on the top and back of one of his shoulders, and some of his ribs were torn out as if done by hogs. His gun, ammunition, and hat were gone. The tracks of the boy were found running and those of some one pursuing, and marks around a tree, as if the little fellow tried to dodge his pursuer. The pursuing tracks were those of a negro. A negro man belonging to Mr. Bibb, who has been in the woods for several months and has lately been seen more than once in that vicinity, is suspected of having committed the fiendish murder and that it was done, too, to get his gun and the ammunition. No pains or expense should be spared to arrest him. Such an outrage is horrible and its commission has very naturally and properly excited much feeling in that moral and orderly community. We deeply sympathize with the afflicted members of the family and hope that condign punishment may soon be visited upon the murderous wretch whose [action] has brought such woe upon them.

The diary of Limestone County resident Thomas Hubbard Hobbs bears an entry dated June 29, 1858: "Porter Bibb's son murdered by his servant."

According to yet another source, Larkin was angry at his master, Porter Bibb—mad enough to kill him. He wanted to take Thomas's hunting rifle to shoot Porter, but a struggle ensued when Thomas refused to give it up readily.

Larkin confessed to the ghastly murder. One might assume that, in the year 1858, he would have been dealt with swiftly and permanently; however, he was taken into custody and tried for murder. On September 13, 1858, Larkin pleaded not guilty. The judge ordered the sheriff to summon "100 good and lawful jurors" to hear the evidence against him. A jury was impaneled to assess the value of Larkin and determine who lawfully owned him before the sentence was passed. It determined that he was worth $1,200 and belonged to Porter Bibb.

Larkin was sentenced to death for the murder of Thomas Bibb. When asked if he had anything further to say, he said nothing. The judge ordered that he be kept in close confinement at the jail until Monday, September 27. Between the hours of 10:00 a.m. and 2:00 p.m., Larkin would be removed from his cell and hanged by the neck "until he be dead within the walls of the jail and no where else." On September 27, 1858, the sentence was carried out.

The tiny Bibb Cemetery, protected by a copse of cedar trees, holds the bodies of members of the Bibb family, including young Thomas. With no words to betray the circumstances of his death, the headstone of Thomas Bibb sums up the tragedy with a simple inscription: "Died in young manhood."

THE BLACK WIDOW
OF HAZEL GREEN

The letter written to a Hazel Green widow from leaders in her Baptist church in Huntsville is now lost to history, as is the exact wording. We do know, however, that there was a letter, and were it written tongue-in-cheek, perhaps it would have read something like this:

Dear Mrs. Elizabeth Dale Gibbons Flanagan Jeffries High Brown Routt,

It has come to our attention that some, if not all, of your many husbands have died under mysterious circumstances and rather prematurely. Though you may explain it as coincidence, we feel that coincidence is not an acceptable theory in our doctrine (authorities are searching for references right now), and some of our members have voiced their concern that sitting too close to you on Sunday mornings puts them in grave (no pun intended) danger of dying due to the collateral effects of possible lightning strike.

Yes, Mrs. Dale Gibbons Flanagan, etc., we know that while your biscuit recipe has been featured in the November issue of *Southern Living* magazine (and we all agree this is historically the best issue of each and every year), no one will eat your biscuits when you bring them to our Fifth Sunday potlucks. Lela Mabel Ann Eliza has suggested that perhaps you have mislabeled your baking powder and rat poison, but we feel you would have probably noticed that after, say, your fourth husband had turned up his toes.

Our minister has conducted so many of your wedding ceremonies that he is sick of wedding reception cheese straws and cannot afford to keep getting his suits dry-cleaned. In fact, the cleaners are not able to get them cleaned fast enough before your next wedding. Our elders have voted, unanimously, that we can no longer accept you as a member of our congregation and that perhaps you would be better suited as a member of the Methodist church down the street. In addition, they seem to have an overabundance of male members of their congregation.

We would like to conclude by wishing any and all future husbands of yours who may be waiting in the wings (sort of like sitting ducks) good luck, but not Godspeed.

Elizabeth Evans Dale was born in Worchester County, Maryland, on October 28, 1795, one of ten children born to Adam Dale and Mary "Polly" Hall. More than two hundred years have passed since her birth, and with the passage of time, memories wither and history forgets. This is not the case for Elizabeth Routt, known locally as the Black Widow of Hazel Green. Though we have details of her life, the answers to many questions will forevermore remain unknown. However, as elusive as the reasons are, her story remains as vivid and interesting as if it happened just yesterday.

In 1797, the Dales left Maryland to settle in Liberty, Dekalb County, Tennessee. In 1812, Adam Dale fought under General Andrew Jackson at the Battle of Horseshoe Bend. He is credited as having raised, equipped and commanded a company of one hundred volunteers from Smith, Tennessee, also in Dekalb County. He and his company camped near a large spring near a small Alabama community called Meridianville. They were just eight miles north of Huntsville and near the future home of his daughter Elizabeth.

It was also in 1812 when seventeen-year-old Elizabeth married twenty-year-old Samuel Gibbons, who was or became a Baptist minister. After eighteen years of marriage, Samuel Gibbons contracted black tongue. He died on June 14, 1830, leaving Elizabeth a widow for the first time at age thirty-five. Elizabeth then moved to Columbia, Tennessee, to be near her brother Edward W., a prominent citizen of that area. Unfortunately, he committed suicide after trouble at the bank where he worked.

Elizabeth remarried fifteen months after her husband's death. Certainly no one was surprised. Men found her charming, and she was notoriously beautiful. Elizabeth was known to be fond of horses and expensive clothing.

Phillip Flanagan, Elizabeth's new husband, was thirty-five-years-old. Their marriage took place on October 3, 1831, but he survived only six months after the wedding. He died on March 14, 1832, and was buried at Maple Hill Cemetery in Huntsville, Alabama.

Nearly nineteen months later, Elizabeth married her third husband, Alexander Jeffries. She was thirty-eight and he was sixty when they exchanged vows on November 6, 1833. Mr. Jeffries owned a plantation near Hazel Green and married Elizabeth eight years after his first wife died.

Hazel Green is a community located four miles from the Tennessee border. By the time the town was incorporated in 1821, there were over three hundred settlers in the community. Hazel Green was a popular and logical resting place for people traveling between Huntsville and Fayetteville.

Jeffries had bought his plantation, located near the Meridian Pike, in 1817 from Archibald Patterson for $1,800. The Jeffries home was built over sacred Indian ground. Locals wondered aloud why he would tempt fate by building on an Indian mound. Located one mile east of Hazel Green, it was situated so that Alexander Jeffries had a sweeping view of the country around the spacious log cabin that was his home. Even with such a wondrous view, the site was strangely spooky. One source claims that the cabin consisted of four rooms, while another claimed there were only two.

This was to be the new home of Elizabeth Dale. The couple had two children: William, who was born in 1834, when Elizabeth was thirty-nine, and Mary Elizabeth, who was born in 1837, when Elizabeth was forty-two.

By February 1838, Alexander Jeffries was not in good health. He called his good friend and neighbor Abner Tate to witness his will. His will provided for his older children from his first wife, while the rest went to Elizabeth and their two children. The will stated that he was of sound mind, though his health was bad.

Seven months later, on September 14, 1838, Alexander Jeffries died at age sixty-five. He was laid to rest in the nearby family cemetery in the shade of holly trees. Next to him was his first wife, Frances, who had died thirteen years earlier. Few people knew of Elizabeth's earlier marriages, and they blamed the death of Alexander on angry Indian spirits.

Eight months after Alexander Jeffries died, forty-four-year-old Elizabeth married again on May 10, 1839. Justice of the Peace J.H. Pierce performed the wedding between Elizabeth Jeffries and Robert High, who was about thirty-nine-years-old. Robert High was well acquainted with marriage, too. Elizabeth was his fourth wife, and he had a seventeen-year-old son named Henry Albert High. The newlyweds lived in Elizabeth's home in Hazel Green.

Husband number four, Robert High, was a native of North Carolina. He was restless and considered to be a dashing widower in the Tuscaloosa social scene, but he went to great pains to cover his bald head. He served as a representative in the state legislature during 1838 and 1839 but spent too much time in the lobby eating apples and peanuts. Unfortunately—but to no one's surprise—he was defeated in the next election.

Just three years after their wedding, Robert High died in 1841, broke and without a will.

To the townspeople, four dead husbands were just too many to accept, and Elizabeth was running out of friends. To complicate matters, Elizabeth had been having problems with her neighbor, Abner Tate.

On August 13, 1844, Elizabeth's daughter Mary died at age seven. Surely her death was attributed to natural causes. Elizabeth waited four years after Robert High's death before marrying again. She married on March 16, 1846, at the age of fifty-one. Her new husband, Absalom Brown, was fifty-two.

Elizabeth Dale Gibbons Flanagan Jeffries High Brown and her new husband built an impressive plantation house on the property purchased by husband number three, Alexander Jeffries. The home, which faced east, consisted of eight large rooms, four upstairs and four downstairs. It replaced the former two-story log cabin built by the late Alexander Jeffries—and yes, it was still on an Indian mound.

It took over a year for a carpenter and slave to build the eight-room, L-shaped mansion, and it became a center for festive parties. But the splendor and gaiety of the Brown plantation came to an end on a night in 1847. Only a year after the marriage, Absalom Brown died of a strange malady, a slow and painful death.

The cause of death was unknown. The unexplained illness was described in the newspaper report of his death as "a malady which caused fast and terrific swelling of his body." Coincidentally—or perhaps not—his corpse resembled the body of a rat after ingesting poison. The poor man was hastily buried that same night under the light of lanterns by Elizabeth's frightened slaves.

On May 11, 1848, a year after Elizabeth lost her fifth husband, Absolom, elder R.H. Taliaferro of the Enon Baptist Church conducted her sixth marriage ceremony to Willis Routt. It was the third ceremony that the suspicious elder conducted for Elizabeth. Willis Routt apparently, and unfortunately for him, put no stock in the rumors about his new bride.

The year 1851 brought sorrow once again to Elizabeth. Her sixth husband died just three years after their marriage. It is interesting to note that family records name only her last three husbands because of the code of etiquette of the time that three trips to the altar were enough for any respectable and decent woman of high quality.

Neighbor Abner Tate was just one of many who became suspicious of the mysterious deaths of Elizabeth's husbands. Their relationship was precarious at best, for they had had several disagreements over loose livestock ruining cotton crops. Elizabeth had sued him for loss of her crops several years earlier and he was not happy with her. Now, Tate was telling anyone and everyone who would listen that he thought she was behind the mysterious deaths of her husbands—and perhaps her daughter's as well.

Abner Tate was doing his farm chores one night in 1854 when he was severely wounded by gunfire. An investigation led them to a slave named Jacob, who belonged to Elizabeth Routt. Tate was convinced that his neighbor Elizabeth was behind the shot, which was meant to be fatal. It was further determined that another slave named Fred was somehow connected as well.

A letter written by Huntsville resident Hugh Lawson Clay to his sister-in-law Virginia, dated June 23, 1854, gives us a possible explanation, as well as a motive. Clay wrote that a runaway slave belonging to Mundford Townsend was staying with Mrs. Routt's slave.

> *This negro of Mrs. R[outt] induced him to shoot T[ate], at his mistress' command, who, he declared, said Tate owed her money, which she had sued him for, but could not get as long as he lived. He furnished Townsend's negro with a double-barreled gun belonging to Wm. Jefferies. This is the substance of the admissions of both negroes and there are corroborative circumstances, in great number and of very strong character, confirmatory of their statements in relation to shooting T[ate], while the absence of all motive for the act except the command of Mrs. R[outt], has brought down upon her the prejudices of the people and revived in strength the rumors of her having made way with six husbands. There is no hope of acquitting either negro. I also think Mrs. R[outt] will be obliged to leave the country.*

Jacob appeared before the Madison County Circuit Court on Tuesday, March 6, 1855. Jacob was arraigned and charged with murder, to which he pleaded not guilty. The jury decided otherwise and found him guilty of murder. It reconvened to assess the dollar value of Jacob on a motion from Jacob's attorney. After placing a value of $925 on Jacob, Judge Thomas A. Walker ordered that the prisoner be returned to jail and reappear before the court the following Friday to receive his sentence.

The minutes of the Madison County Circuit Court, dated Saturday, March 10, 1855, record that Jacob was brought once again to the bar, and although he was given the chance to speak, he declined to comment. It was ordered that he remain in prison until Friday, March 30, at which time he would be hanged in or near Huntsville, between the hours of noon and 2:00 p.m.

According to a short paragraph in the Wednesday, March 14, 1855 *Southern Advocate*, many people believed that Elizabeth was behind the plot, although she was never formally charged. Jacob's accused accomplice, Fred, died in jail before he could be brought to trial. D.H. Bingham, a schoolteacher in Meridianville and Elizabeth Routt's new suitor, stated that Fred gave a statement just before he died that contradicted all of his previous confessions. On his deathbed, Fred stated, "God knows I had nothing to do with shooting Mr. Tate."

The April 4, 1855 edition of the *Southern Advocate* announced that the execution had been carried out. On Monday, April 9, the State of Alabama paid $426.50 to Elizabeth for half the value of Jacob, her executed slave.

Long after Jacob's sentence was carried out, Abner Tate and Elizabeth Routt continued their campaign of slander, slinging accusations in court and other public venues. The culmination of Jacob's trial was only a small subplot in the bizarre story of two people bent on revenge. Bad blood between Elizabeth Routt and Abner Tate only got worse.

Now sixty years old, Elizabeth persuaded her new suitor to accuse Abner Tate of murder, concocting a bizarre story that resulted in a sensational trial. Tate was tried for murdering a man sixteen years earlier, and it was suggested that he had murdered a second man. His trial began on the last day of December 1855 and finished on Friday, January 4, 1856. He was found innocent.

After the trial, Abner Tate paid Huntsville novelist (and cousin to Mark Twain) Jeremiah Clemens to write a salacious pamphlet against Elizabeth Routt and D.H. Bingham. Tate acknowledged that he paid $500 to Clemens to write the fifty-six-page document. This was Tate's public defense against the slanderous accusations by Elizabeth Routt and the new man in her life, D.H. Bingham.

The booklet written by Jeremiah Clemens was filled with venom and spite. One excerpt claimed that around Elizabeth's marriage bed,

> *six grinning skeletons were already hung…[She] was entitled to all the consolation an industrious sober man can bring to the bed around which nightly assembles a conclave of ghosts to witness the endearments that once*

were theirs and shudder through their fleshless forms at the fiendish spirit which wraps the grave worm in the bridal garment and infused a lingering death with a conjugal kiss.

Bingham was livid about the pamphlet, in which he was mentioned numerous times. He was not about to let the accusations against him go unanswered. An excerpt of Bingham's response, written to the *Athens Herald*, states:

> *It is known that he (Tate) is illiterate and scarcely able to put together three consecutive lines in the English language; while the pamphlet exhibits in its arrangement and details professional skill and tact.*
>
> *It is written by the one (Clemens) to whom rumor attributes it, he is a man of intellect, genius, and talent; naturally towering, lofty and noble, capable of wielding the scepter of an Empire, mentally; and were his mental qualifications backed and sustained by a moral courage and integrity of purpose, sufficient to resist those inebriating excitant that debase his lofty genius and bring it down to the groveling level of those who bow and cringe for hire, at the shrine of mannon, he would be morally worthy of wearing the proudest diadem within the gift of the enlightened people of this fair Republic.*

Bingham continued with his explanation:

> *Having succeeded in obtaining an acquittal, they were not satisfied in letting the matter rest, but in the excess of their joy, made a publication in which the facts of the case were grossly perverted, falsified and misrepresented the character of witness and prosecutor grossly vilified.*

Still, there was the matter of Elizabeth's serial widowhood. She had already gained the attention of a number of people for the sudden and mysterious deaths of her many husbands, and the church had withdrawn her membership. While others whispered their suspicions about Elizabeth, Abner Tate blatantly accused her of murdering her husbands.

A complaint was filed on August 9, 1856. Elizabeth E. Routt sued Abner Tate for $50,000 for the publication of his pamphlet entitled *Defense of Abner Tate against Charges of Murder Preferred by D.A. Bingham*.

But the trial never took place. The suit was dismissed because Elizabeth had already moved to Marshall County, Mississippi, and sold her plantation to Levi Donaldson for $12,500. Defendant Abner Tate asked that the court dismiss the charges and that he recover any costs incurred from Mrs. Routt. The court agreed to consider the motion.

In 1860, Abner Tate moved to south Alabama, just before the outbreak of the Civil War. As far as history books are concerned, the mystery of the missing men he was accused of killing has never been explained.

Elizabeth was described as a fascinating lady of many marriages. Folklore says that she had a hatrack near her door that displayed one hat from each of her dead husbands.

Elizabeth had the body of her first husband removed from Centerville, Tennessee, and taken to Columbia. His interesting tombstone is in the shape of a pulpit with an open Bible on top.

The personal feud of two people, supposedly started by loose livestock, destroyed reputations and fortunes and caused the deaths of two slaves. All that remains of the mystery today is found in the pages of court records, the ruins of the plantation home destroyed by arson in 1968 and a small, crowded graveyard under an immense holly tree one mile east of Hazel Green. The steps and remnants of three fireplaces are all that is left of the home of the notoriously beautiful Elizabeth Routt. Did she kill her six husbands? This much we do know: Elizabeth took the truth with her when she died.

A JOKE ON MADISON COUNTY

It all started as a joke. Eight friends in New Hope and Poplar Ridge thought it would be great sport to promote a local tenant farmer, forty-two-year-old Oliver "Highpockets" McPeters (also known as "Mac"), in the run for sheriff of Madison County. McPeters was a funny guy and not at all educated, but enough money was scraped together to pay the $60.00 required for a filing fee. Another $7.84 was thrown in for campaign cards and a little advertising. McPeters didn't own a suit, and his shoes had seen better days, so he bought himself a politicking outfit on credit. With that taken care of, he was off to the races.

The year 1950 was a big one for the office of sheriff of Madison County. A number of men threw their hats into the ring. The eight men who backed Oliver McPeters required only that he campaign and attend rallies. But there was another problem: McPeters didn't own a vehicle. At times, he hitched a ride with friends to rallies, but the rest of the time, he was on his own to find a ride. And so he did the only thing he could do: he hitchhiked. One time he arrived at a rally just in time for it to be over. His excuse was delivered with a good ol' boy grin: "Not too many cars on the road tonight."

McPeters's platform was semireligious, and as such, he promised a thorough cleanup of the honky-tonks in the county. He didn't have any experience, as his opponents were quick to point out, but he countered by saying that those who had the experience hadn't done their jobs while in office. "Give a poor man a chance" became his campaign slogan.

While his friends in New Hope and Poplar Ridge snickered at McPeters's success, he took his campaign seriously. The lanky man pushed away the microphone when it was his turn to speak. Standing with his hands on his hips, he reared back and shouted to the crowd like a Baptist minister. Most campaigning in those days was done on a soapbox. There were no television spots, no radio advertisements and rarely an ad in the newspaper. Wherever there was a crowd and a politician, you had yourself a political rally.

To the surprise of everyone, Oliver McPeters made it into the runoff, upsetting three incumbents. The practical joke had taken on a life of its own, and while he was in second place in the first heat, he broke out in the lead and was elected, beating the favorite, Floyd Green, by 502 votes for a total of 3,780. His "poor man platform" brought a surprising number of folks from the rural areas of Madison County to vote for one of their own and help put the honky-tonks out of business.

The swearing-in was scheduled for January 14, 1951. The newly elected sheriff of Madison County announced to the good citizens that, effective January 15, he was going after the moonshiners in the county. It was going to be a new day for the people of Madison County.

McPeters's announcement that day shared the news in the *Huntsville Times* with a story about the ladies of the United Daughters of the Confederacy up in Richmond, Virginia. Twelve cannonballs had been stolen from a display, and the ladies just knew it had to be the work of Yankees. They compared the loss to the legendary Scottish Stone of Scone, stolen by the British.

Although Sheriff Oliver McPeters was new to the political arena, there were some aspects of the job that he took to like a duck to water. Even before he took the oath to uphold the integrity of the law, etc., he had already lined up his bribes. He made an oral agreement with the various fraternal and veterans organizations to allow them to keep slot machines and the like for a fee. In return, he would shut down all other gaming places in the county and give them a heads-up whenever the feds planned a raid. Another exception was made for Joe's Place, a local roadhouse known for dice tables and illegal whiskey.

All was well for the first few months. A slot machine maintenance man, representing a number of clubs in town, was responsible for collecting the payoffs. According to records, the agreed-upon sum of $1,000 would be enough to ensure that law enforcement would look the other way. But the sheriff got greedy. Before long, he raised his demands to $50 per week, then $65 per week and finally $125 per week. His greed was his undoing. Some of the bribes were paid by check, and in fact the exalted ruler of the Elks Club made out his check with the word "bribe" in the notation line. But Sheriff McPeters perhaps didn't notice; he could neither read nor write, and he endorsed his checks with a simple "X." One source says that the final straw came when an unannounced federal raid shut down those gambling facilities and someone turned him in anonymously.

To say the least, the sheriff's political career was short-lived. McPeters made the headlines of the *Huntsville Times* on August 17, 1951. "Sheriff's Impeachment Asked," the huge headline announced, and the story explained that the county grand jury had recommended to Circuit Judge Elbert Parsons that McPeters be tried on charges of corruption and moral turpitude. In spite of his limited education, those were words he did not want to hear.

His impeachment case would be heard before the state supreme court, the newspaper announced, and then the state's case would be heard by the attorney general's office. Evidence showed that the sheriff had received $100 in early January, $400 in February, $300 in April and so forth, until he had pocketed $965 total. His explanation to the public was classically simple, "You know I've always tried to be a good boy."

During McPeters's trial, he continued to deny that he was accepting bribes. He claimed that he had asked for a $1,000 loan from the slot machine maintenance man and that he was purely innocent. The court decided differently. On November 13, 1951, Sheriff Oliver McPeters, a country boy from one of the most rural sections of Madison County, once again made the headlines in the *Huntsville Times*. "McPeters Ousted as Sheriff," screamed the headline announcing the outcome of his trial. Madison County coroner Bob Rigsby was automatically chosen to fill the vacancy in the sheriff's office until an appointment could be made.

Sheriff McPeters did not go quietly into the night. "I went into the office of sheriff a poor man and I am going out a poor man," he announced. He also hinted that the good citizens of Madison County had not seen the last of him. He might just run again someday.

Some folks felt sorry for the sheriff. Perhaps he wasn't aware of what was happening or maybe he was set up. But then again, corruption in politics was nothing new.

Oliver McPeters died on March 25, 1986, at age seventy-seven. His wife had preceded him in death, and he was laid to rest next to her at the historic Bethel Cemetery near the Poplar Ridge community. His grave, located in the northwest corner of the beautiful graveyard, lies just above a ridge, protectively covered by a number of old trees. At last, in death, Sheriff Oliver McPeters has found some dignity.

PURE AS THE DRIVEN SLUSH
ALABAMA'S TALLULAH BANKHEAD

The people of Alabama practically demanded that the role of Scarlett O'Hara in *Gone With the Wind* go to Huntsville native Tallulah Bankhead. She was a bona fide movie star and, most importantly, a southern girl. But misbehavior was her oxygen, and her reputation, even by Hollywood standards, was downright legendary.

Tallulah had few, if any, inhibitions. The story was told that she was intently listening to Eleanor Roosevelt while the two visited in the proximity of a bathroom. Not bothering to excuse herself or close the door, she simply dropped drawers and sat on the toilet without interrupting the first lady's conversation.

Perhaps she had a reason to crave attention. Tallulah Brockman Bankhead was born on January 31, 1902, to a ravishing beauty, Adelaide Eugenia Bankhead, in Huntsville, Alabama. Her mother died from blood poisoning as a result of childbirth complications a few weeks later. Adelaide's mother had died the same way. Adelaide was from a prominent Mississippi family and was engaged to marry. While visiting one of her bridesmaids in Huntsville, she met attorney William Bankhead. It was love at first sight. Adelaide's engagement was called off, and she married Bankhead instead.

William Bankhead and his family were steeped in southern politics. Democrats to the bone, William served as Speaker of the House; her uncle, John H. Bankhead II and her grandfather, John H. Bankhead, were both senators.

At first, fate seemed to smile on Will and Adelaide Bankhead. Daughter Eugenie was born, followed a year later by Tallulah, who was named for her grandmother. According to legend, Tallulah's grandmother was conceived while her parents were staying at Tallulah Falls in Georgia. After bearing two daughters, the radiant wife of Will Bankhead was dead, leaving him emotionally devastated and in a downward spiral.

Tallulah and her sister, Eugenie, were taken to Jasper, Alabama, where their grandparents lived. For the rest of their youth, they were raised alternately in Jasper; in Washington, D.C.; and by various paternal relatives—an aunt, their grandparents and occasionally even their father. Bankhead remarried a few years later and once caught young Tallulah mimicking her stepmother. He told her the only place for that behavior was on the theatre stage. So began her acting career.

At age fifteen, Tallulah pestered her grandmother to let her submit a photograph to a movie magazine for a beauty contest. Her photograph was chosen among the finalists, but she had failed to send in her name and address. She was not an attractive child, and members of her family hoped that perhaps a rejection from the magazine would clear her head. The plan backfired, and when she made up her mind to try the theatre in New York, her aunt agreed to be her chaperone.

Tallulah eventually made her way to the London stage, where she was a sensation for a number of years. Her outrageous lifestyle was already drawing attention. She was investigated for corruption of several Eton schoolboys by engaging them in indecent and unnatural sex acts. Charges were never brought against her.

Tallulah once turned cartwheels at a party, sans underwear. She welcomed guests at her door during one of her parties with her ever-present cigarette holder in her hand but no clothing. A startled guest was surprised to see that everyone carried on around her as if nothing were out of the ordinary. One of her very straight-laced elderly friends commented to an unhinged guest, "I don't know why Tallulah goes around naked, she has so many pretty frocks."

Tallulah insisted on punctuality when guests were invited to her home, yet she once forgave a male guest for being hours late because he brought her flowers he had decorated by hand. It seems that the man bought tulips and then decided that some needed stripes and others needed polka dots. He applied the stripes and polka dots with paint and then waited for them to dry before showing up at Tallulah's home.

Tallulah bought herself a Bentley even though she had not yet learned to drive. Her sense of direction was worse than her driving, however, and she would call a taxi to lead the way from one point to another while she followed behind.

Huntsville native Tallulah Bankhead.

Away from the prying eyes of her strict southern family, Tallulah drank to excess, had sex to excess and took drugs. When she went on days-long drinking binges, she would not eat food, and when it came to sex, she slept with men and/ or women. Her promiscuity finally caught up with her. After several abortions before the age of thirty, she nearly died from advanced venereal disease, which necessitated an emergency hysterectomy.

Tallulah was one of the many actresses who wanted desperately to snag the role of Scarlett O'Hara, based on the nation's bestselling book *Gone With the Wind*. Tallulah excelled in her screen test, but because she was thirty-six years old, all were concerned that she would not pass for the very young Scarlett in the beginning barbecue scene. It was the right part but the wrong time. When Tallulah heard that young Shirley Temple was filmed through gauze, she said, "I should be filmed through linoleum."

Tallulah never forgot her Alabama roots, though she didn't get home very often. In 1937, she flew home with fellow actor John Emery. They were married at the Bankhead home known as Sunset, while crowds of fans waited outside the gates to get a glimpse of the stars. There were problems in the marriage early on, however. Her career eclipsed his, and their time spent apart exceeded their time together. No one was surprised when it ended. Although the marriage was long over, it was legally ended after four years.

Sources differ regarding Tallulah's feelings about her mother's premature death. Some say that she felt guilty and visited her mother's grave only once, while other sources say that, although she would always wonder about her mother, she did not blame herself. One interesting story, though unauthenticated, bears repeating. Tallulah attended a séance in Hollywood, and in the course of the evening, she was visited by her mother's ghost. Through a spiritual advisor, Tallulah was asked to realign her mother's headstone at Huntsville's Maple Hill Cemetery. Some days or weeks later, Tallulah called a family friend in Huntsville to look into the status of the headstone. As it turned out, the small obelisk was askew over the square base. Tallulah was unnerved by the news and did not participate in another séance.

Tallulah's father died after months of poor health in the early fall of 1940. Although he had long since remarried after the death of his first wife, everyone, including his second wife, knew that the love of his life was buried in Huntsville's Maple Hill Cemetery. He had agreed, however, that when the time came, he would be buried in Jasper instead of Huntsville. Adelaide Eugenia Bankhead remains buried alone at Maple Hill, with not a single member of her family nearby.

Over the years, Tallulah became increasingly difficult for others to work with. She was a loose cannon and a difficult diva. She suffered from insecurities about her acting ability, perhaps because she never had formal acting lessons. Even so, she had a style that was emulated by many other actresses. She did not care to act in movies because they were filmed out of sequence, and she found it difficult to conjure emotions when at times she was speaking to no one. The theatre was much more realistic.

Tallulah took her last role for fun. In 1967, she played a very camp black widow in the *Batman* television series. But her health was already failing, and her exquisite beauty was gone. Bad habits, fostered over her lifetime, shortened her time on earth. She smoked one hundred cigarettes per day, drank and took illegal drugs, and she could not, or would not, take the steps to help herself. Toward the end, she paid someone to hold her hand at night until she fell asleep.

On December 12, 1968, legendary actress Tallulah Bankhead died in a New York City hospital of double pneumonia, complicated by chronic emphysema. It was worsened by malnutrition due to a prolonged drinking binge. According to several sources, her last words were: "Codeine, bourbon." Tallulah was buried at Saint Paul's Church in Chestertown, Maryland, far from her Alabama home.

THE TRIAL OF THE CENTURY

On the morning of April 17, 1884, spectators filled a Huntsville courtroom, craning their necks to see the famous defendant in his stylish Prince Albert coat. The prisoner appeared to be older than his years, and his hair was thinning. His large ears stood straight out from his head, and he was gaunt and pale. Only a few members of the crowd were women, among them the distraught wife of the defendant, who sat quietly with her six-year-old son. The man who stood trial that day was not from Huntsville, but he was well known indeed. Frank James, brother and fellow outlaw of Jesse James, was accused of robbing Alexander Smith, a government paymaster, near Muscle Shoals, Alabama, three years earlier.

The twelve men of the jury were described by the local reporter as "a very fair looking body, most of them evidently from the country." They were white men, of course, for women and black men were assumed not to be intelligent enough to understand legal terminology. The attorneys were celebrities as well. The chief prosecutor was former Alabama governor William H. Smith, and the chief defense attorney was former Confederate secretary of war Leroy P. Walker. Both attorneys were famous for high drama in the courtroom. The spectators hoped they would not be disappointed. It was rumored that one or more Confederate veterans' organizations were chipping in for Frank James's legal defense.

Jesse and Frank James were credited with having committed many crimes in their lifetimes. Most likely, they were responsible for only a fraction of those crimes; others were attributed to them because it was convenient to do so. During the Civil War, the two brothers had ridden with Quantrill's

Frank James.

Raiders, widely known for their bloodthirsty raids in and around Missouri. Although the raiders' sympathies leaned toward the Southern cause, for the most part they remained unsanctioned by the Confederate government. They rode by their own rules and answered to no man.

Not much is known of their lives during the decade after the Civil War. It is believed that from about 1875 until 1881, Frank and Jesse lived quiet lives with their families near Nashville. Jesse took the alias Tom Howard, and Frank was known as Ben Woodson. They were recognized as fine judges of horse flesh and respectable citizens who left home for unexplained, and protracted, periods of time. But a foray into Alabama changed all that.

The paymaster for the U.S. Army Corps of Engineers, a Scotsman named Alexander "Alleck" Smith, was assigned to a project to deepen a shallow stretch of the Muscle Shoals. On the chilly, rainy day of March 11, 1881, Smith started his ride to Campbell's Bank in Florence, Alabama, to pick up the workers' weekly payroll, which had been issued from a bank in Chattanooga. With more than $5,000 in gold, silver and currency packed into his saddlebags, Smith began the twenty-mile trip back to camp. He was not comfortable carrying so much money with him, or having to travel alone, but after all, it was his job. Smith stepped off his horse at Douglass's Gate near Lock 5. From out of nowhere, three bearded men wearing slouch hats appeared, with pistols aimed directly at his head. The bandits took the money from the saddlebags, along with his pistol, and had Smith accompany them as they took back roads headed due north. Along the way, they politely urged him to ride faster and expressed concern for his well-being.

Alexander Smith wondered if he had lived his last day on earth. Somewhere near Bull's Mill, the riders found a secluded area under the cover of trees and ordered Smith to dismount. His knees buckled as he stepped off his horse onto the wet ground. The three bearded men divided up the bounty and then, surprisingly, handed Smith his own watch and returned to him his own money. (Here, accounts differ. It seems that somewhere between thirty-one and fifty dollars were his to begin with.) One robber explained that they only wanted U.S. money and did not wish to rob him personally. The bandits had spoken to him kindly, gave him an overcoat and apologized for not furnishing him with rubber overalls to shield him from the rain.

Storm clouds rumbled in the darkening sky as cold sheets of rain began to fall to the ground. Smith was instructed to remain there until morning as the bandits rode off into the safety of the gathering darkness.

On the following day, Alexander Smith arrived at the work camp and told his harrowing story. Posses were quickly assembled and thundered off in different directions, hoping to pick up the trail of the robbers. Unfortunately for them, all remnants of possible clues had been erased by the pounding rain.

There are several versions of what happened next. According to a story in the *New York Times*, one of the known James Gang members, William Ryan, rode out of Nashville on a main road a few weeks later, half drunk and making a scene. He waved his pistol dangerously, bragging that there was not a man alive who could take him. The justice of the peace waited until Ryan fell into a drunken slumber and then arrested him. In Ryan's possession was $1,660 found in the wrappings of the Chattanooga bank. Frank, Jesse and another gang member, Dick Liddle, left the state as soon as they heard about the arrest.

Another version differs only slightly. A man who gave his name as Tom Hill wandered into a saloon in Whites Creek, Tennessee, and after downing a number of glasses of whiskey, he became belligerent. When he drew his pistol, silence blanketed the room. After a struggle, Tom Hill was strong-armed into submission and turned over to the police. Almost $1,500 in gold coins were found to be in his possession. Tom Hill, alias Jack Ryan, alias Whiskey Head Ryan, was none other than William Ryan, a member of the notorious gang of outlaws who rode with Jesse James.

The election of a new governor in Missouri brought with it the promise of law and order in the state. A huge reward was offered for Frank and Jesse James, inspiring Bob Ford, a member of Jesse's own gang, to shoot Jesse in the back of the head on April 3, 1882, for the reward money. Fearing for the safety of his family, Frank James surrendered to Missouri governor T.T. Crittenden himself.

After his acquittal in Missouri on other charges, Frank James was extradited to Alabama to face charges for the payroll robbery. According to some accounts, residents of Huntsville welcomed Frank James as a celebrity when he arrived in October 1883. Fans checked him out of jail to join them for a home-cooked meal, and Limestone County resident William Hundley checked James out to accompany him on a bird hunt. Others sent flowers and fruit to the prisoner. In spite of the gay mood of the residents, one letter home indicates that Frank James was less than impressed with the people of Huntsville.

From the Huntsville jail, James wrote to his wife in Kearney, Missouri, on March 6, 1884:

> *My Dear Wife and Rob,*
>
> *The chances for bond has failed. No one here are willing to do any thing unless the amount of bond is placed on deposit in this place which is $5,000 so I have told them they can all go to the devil. We have always said that the meanest people on Earth live South and we was not wrong about it either. Should an other war ever come in my day and time I would march with my sword against them and I haven't words to express my contempt for each people of course there are many good people here but it is among that poor class. You never saw a capitalist in your life that was not mean. You never will either. I am feeling quite well today and will make up my mind to stick it out until April when I will be acquitted and then they can all go to the devil. I hope you and Rob are well. Write me when you feel like it. Love to all, I am your affectionate husband, Frank James.*

One of Frank James's visitors was a quiet preacher named William Clark McCoy, from nearby Sand Mountain, who asked to pray with the prisoner alone. A look of surprised recognition appeared on Frank's face as the stranger walked in.

"Bill, they said you was dead!" Frank said in surprise.

The preacher quickly put his index finger to his lips, indicating the urgent need for Frank's silence. The two men talked in low voices for an hour before the preacher took his leave. Frank watched him walk out. Whatever the two men discussed was never revealed. There had already been rumors that the preacher was none other than Bill Quantrill, the leader of Quantrill's Raiders. Officially, he was listed as having died at the hands of Yankees in 1865. Others believed that he was captured, spent the remainder of the war in Elmira Prison and, upon his release, made his way into Alabama, where he took up a new life and a new identity. The real Quantrill was known to be a crack shot with a pistol or rifle, and no one who knew of his reputation dared to push the subject for fear of death.

Some historians hold the federal government responsible for forcing members of the James Gang into lives of crime. Frank James was self-taught and had wanted to attend college, but at the outbreak of the Civil War, he enlisted with the Missouri State Guard, fighting for the Confederacy. He joined Quantrill's Raiders when he was nineteen. At the end of the war, all Confederate troops were pardoned, but an exception was made for members of guerilla bands. They would not be pardoned and were expected to answer for their crimes against the Union. Quantrill's Raiders fell squarely into that category. In an effort to turn his life around, James signed an oath of allegiance after the war and tried to surrender in Lexington, Missouri, but he was fired at by soldiers and escaped. Members of the Pinkerton Detective Agency tried on several occasions to capture the outlaws, resulting in the death of several agents. According to one source, Pinkerton agents threw an incendiary bomb into the home of the James brothers. Their mother was badly burned, and their much younger half brother was killed.

The trial in Huntsville was news all over the country. The three robbers were believed to be the same men who wandered around the Muscle Shoals work camp claiming to be with the revenue service and/or fruit tree salesmen. Several witnesses for the prosecution could not positively identify Frank James as one of the men in question. Even Alexander Smith couldn't be absolutely sure. The key witness for the prosecution, Dick Liddle, also a member of the James Gang looking for a deal, could not be considered a reliable witness because he had been an outlaw himself.

There were other witnesses who swore that they saw Frank James in Nashville on the day of the alleged robbery. When the case was handed over to the jury of twelve men, they took a total of five hours to deliberate and deliver their verdict. Not surprisingly, Frank James was acquitted, but he would not be a free man. Unbeknownst to each other, two sheriffs, one from Missouri and another from Minnesota, waited quietly for the outcome of the trial. Both expected to escort James, if he was acquitted, back to their respective states to stand trial on other charges. The sheriff from Missouri put his hand on James first and took his prisoner into custody.

When one of the members of the jury was questioned later, he admitted that although James was probably guilty, under the letter of the law, the jury could not be sure beyond the shadow of a doubt. In the first round of ballots, three men voted for a guilty verdict and the rest for acquittal. After a discussion, the three holdouts were convinced that they, too, should vote for acquittal.

Later in life, Frank James took on odd jobs to support himself and his family. He worked as a doorman, usher and bouncer at the Standard Theatre Saloon in St. Louis and became a shoe salesman and farmer. He joined fellow outlaw Cole Younger in a traveling Wild West show and finally settled at the family farm in Missouri to give tours of the James home for twenty-five cents per person.

The relationship between Frank James and his wife appears, in retrospect, to have been one of great love and admiration. Anna was ten years younger than her husband and had earned a degree in science and literature from the Independence Female College. She was adept with horses and knew how to fire a pistol with deadly accuracy. She would not be photographed or interviewed. Anna eloped with Frank in 1874, with full knowledge of his career as an outlaw. When her family found out much later who Frank really was, they disowned Anna. But she understood and apparently accepted the circumstances. Frank and Anna enjoyed fine literature and Shakespeare. They attended the theatre in large cities, and they remained devoted to each other until Frank's death.

In 1915, Frank James died at the age of seventy-two. His body was cremated, and his ashes were kept in a bank vault until 1944, when his wife died. They were both buried at Hill Park Cemetery in Independence. Today, the James Farm is a tourist attraction, as is the Liberty, Missouri bank believed to be the first bank robbed by the James brothers. With help from the James brothers, it was relieved of $62,000 and forced to close due to insufficient funds.

The relationship between the town of Huntsville, Alabama, and the family of Frank James did not end in the year 1884. Some fourteen years later, his son Robert, who was a lad of six when he arrived for his father's trial in 1884, came to Huntsville once again. This time, though, the circumstances were much different. As a private in Troop G, Second Cavalry, Robert James served as a bodyguard to General Coppinger. They were among the several thousand men sent to Huntsville to recover from yellow fever after the Spanish-American War. Hopefully, he found the residents of Huntsville to be much more gracious than did his infamous father.

DAVID HUMPHREYS TODD
THE PRESIDENT'S BROTHER-IN-LAW

President Lincoln married into a family that would become divided by the Civil War. Many of them called to him when they were in trouble and then cursed him in public, causing him immeasurable heartache and embarrassment. The pro-Southern branch of the clan used Selma as their base. But it was David Todd, perhaps one of the most notorious of the family, who eventually made Huntsville, Alabama, his home.

David was the fourth child born to his father's second wife. His half sister Mary was fourteen years his senior. When she married Abe Lincoln, David was only ten years old. He left home at age fifteen and fought in the Mexican War. Although his father had hoped he would learn discipline while in the army, he seemed to learn the other aspects of army life—cursing, drinking and gambling—more thoroughly. As a child of privilege and wealth, David developed a drinking problem that would plague him throughout his life.

With the beginning of the bloody War Between the States in 1861, the Todd family found themselves separated by conflicting sympathies, magnified by Mary's famous husband. Lieutenant David Todd was an aide to General Theophilus Holmes in Richmond about the time of the Battle of Manassas. Without warning, there was a sudden need to house nearly fifteen hundred Union prisoners, and the city was unprepared. Todd was sent to work under General John Winder, who was in charge of Richmond security, and by default, it was his job to make sure that the prisoners were taken care of. David became the commandant of the emptied tobacco warehouses that would become their horrifying new home.

Mary Todd Lincoln, half sister of David Humphreys Todd.

The citizens of Richmond gathered to make fun of the prisoners and shower them with insults, escalating the anti-Union sentiments even further. These actions did not translate well to those responsible for the prisoners' well-being.

Todd complained that he preferred to be in the throes of battle, and he was reported to have been especially cruel to the inmates. To make matters worse, the camp was terribly overcrowded, and because it was early in the war, there had not yet been an established prisoner exchange. Still, one has to wonder how much can be attributed to Todd's relationship to the president. He was certainly watched more closely, as some people must have wondered whether he was a spy for the Union in a gray uniform. Some have argued that he was intensely cruel to prove his allegiance to the South.

There were several eyewitness accounts of Todd's unnecessary cruelty. Several sources tell of the time he walked into the inmate population with his sword drawn, indiscriminately stabbing one or more men and then casually ordering medical aid for them as he walked out with blood on his sword.

Because there were no bars on the upper-floor windows, Todd ordered that anyone who stuck a head or hand out of the open window of the prison would be shot. Bored guards waited for an opportunity to shoot; three men were reported to have been killed and many others wounded. Todd knew that although he didn't actually pull the trigger, he was ultimately responsible, so he rescinded the order. Some sources claim that he was constantly drunk throughout his tenure with the prison system.

It was another incident that ended his two-month reign over the prison. One night, several guards came to his quarters carrying a dead Union soldier. They put the body down in order to knock on Todd's door. Todd had been drinking—which was not that unusual—and was incensed when he opened the door to find a dead Yankee on his doorstep. In fury, he kicked the Union corpse out into the street, where it remained until the next day. That was too much for his commander, and even the pro-Confederate public, to swallow. His conduct that night became a nationwide scandal. Still, no matter how outrageous his actions were reported to be, none could come close to those of his assistant in Richmond, Henry Wirz, who became the commandant of the notorious Andersonville Prison in Georgia. For his wartime atrocities, Wirz was hanged.

By this time, David Todd was already suffering from consumption, an old-time name for the almost always fatal and highly contagious disease known as tuberculosis. In the summer of 1861, he called on two imprisoned Union surgeons to treat him during one of his hemorrhagic episodes. They walked into his room to find that he had coughed up enormous amounts of blood and it had splattered everywhere. When he regained his strength a week later, Todd invited the prisoners to his room for a lavish dinner to show his appreciation. It was apparent to the surgeons that he had been entertaining female company, and one of the doctors cautioned him about the danger of his "unnecessary activity." He informed the surgeon that he was not born to die in his bed.

Still, David Todd remained in the service of the Confederate army. He kept in touch with his sisters in Selma, but there was no known contact with his sister in the White House. While Todd was embroiled in the siege of Vicksburg, there was a rumor that he had been fatally wounded. Mary Lincoln wrote to another sibling that even if it were not true, he was dead to her, as if he had joined the Confederate army simply to personally embarrass her. It was no wonder that Abraham Lincoln was said to have commented that one "d" was good enough for God but not good enough for the Todds. Historians agree that Mary saw herself as the center of the universe.

The story of Todd's death has been misreported by historians for years and perpetuated, unintentionally, by members of his own family. Newspapers reported that he was shot at Vicksburg and was thought by some to have died on the spot or shortly thereafter. Another version said that he was shot through the lung, and although he survived for a time, it was his ordeal at Vicksburg that caused him to die prematurely. Whatever the case, he wrote to his mother after his time spent at Vicksburg and reported that he had survived without a scratch.

The rumor of having been wounded in his lung was not exactly without merit, though the facts were somewhat skewed. At any rate, David Todd spent much time in and around Selma, and it was perhaps during one of his furloughs when he met Susan Turner Williamson, a widow from Huntsville. In the waning days of the devastating war, the couple celebrated their matrimony on April 4, 1865, in Marion, Alabama. In just a few days, General Robert E. Lee met with General Ulysses Grant at Appomattox to surrender on behalf of the Confederate army. Only a few days later, David Todd's famous brother-in-law, President Abraham Lincoln, died from an assassin's bullet. One must wonder if David Todd, at that time, regretted the words he had uttered time and time again about wanting to cut Abe Lincoln's heart out with his own sword.

The newlyweds' Huntsville home, which is no longer standing, was located in the Twickenham Historic District. Todd was a shopkeeper in his father-in-law's business and led a relatively quiet life for the next few years.

In 1869, however, members of Congress began an investigation into prison abuse during the Civil War. David Todd's name came up. Because Henry Wirz and Todd had been linked early on, they were naturally compared to each other. One former prisoner's recollection seemed to sum them up: "[Henry] Wirz killed to please his superiors; [David] Todd [killed] from personal delight in human blood and suffering." Another prisoner speculated that, had Todd been in charge of Andersonville, the suffering and death would have been far greater.

David Todd's attempt to reestablish himself was short-lived. Tuberculosis claimed his life on Sunday, July 30, 1871, at age thirty-nine. His funeral was conducted in Huntsville's beautiful Church of Nativity, and his burial took place nearby at Maple Hill Cemetery. His wife, widowed now for a second time, did not remain in Huntsville.

One of the Union surgeons who had treated him early in the war heard of his death and commented that, although he *did* die in his bed, "he waited altogether too long before doing it."

Over the years, the ravages of time took a toll on David Todd's headstone, the last remaining indicator of his life, and ultimate death, in Huntsville. The flat stone over his grave lay in the path of a growing magnolia tree. The roots of the magnolia, which tend to grow exposed near the surface of the ground, proved to be mightier than the stone. Todd's headstone was split and broken, and eventually the pieces were discarded. In 2004, however, a Confederate stone was re-erected over the grave of David Humphreys Todd. Good or bad, Abraham Lincoln's notorious brother-in-law is once again remembered.

Huntsville's Famous Madam

W hatever you do, do it the best you can," our elders tell us, "for no matter what you choose to do in life, there is no shame in a job well done." Those words carry the unspoken assumption that we will choose to do something legal—better yet, honorable—and our great works will in some way help or inspire mankind. But sometimes life happens to us, and circumstances direct us onto a different path. Perhaps that was the case for Mollie Teal, Huntsville's most well-known madam.

Mollie Teal's life before Huntsville is as mysterious as her death. Some sources indicate that she spent time in Tennessee, others say Montgomery. She was born less than a decade before the start of the Civil War, and perhaps in the dark and desperate years after the war, she turned to the one profession in which she knew she could make a living. Whatever the feelings about her at the time, history has remembered her for her benevolence to the city that she eventually called home.

Mollie Teal was, among other things, a successful and shrewd businesswoman. Most of her girls were young transients, who perhaps turned to prostitution as a last resort. Mollie took care of them, had them examined by doctors on a regular basis and dressed them well. At any given time, she employed about fifteen to twenty girls. They stayed at Mollie's establishment for only a short time, usually weeks or months, before moving on. Though they were much appreciated by the men in town, they were not allowed to sit down or eat ice cream in the local drugstore, and if they went to the Elks Theatre to see a show on stage, they were required to enter through an alley and sit in special seats reserved just for them. More than one of Mollie's beautiful girls married into prominent Huntsville families, causing much social embarrassment when they encountered other prominent former customers in the parlors of proper folks' homes.

It wasn't long before Mollie was able to buy a large house from Oscar Hundley (listed in the city directory as a "capitalist") for $300 cash. It was a large house on the corner of present-day Gallatin and St. Clair Streets. Mollie took out bank loans from time to time to update and remodel the home, but it never took her long to repay the loans in full. Unlike most homes in town, Miss Mollie's had an indoor bathroom.

Mollie invested money in her hometown. On June 9, 1892, she bought a share of stock in the Dallas Mill, and a few days later, she bought another. She was known to donate money when it went toward a good cause—and why not? Fleeting as the moment was, it may have been the only time she got respect.

The fees in Mollie's establishment were easy to remember. It was a standard two dollars for every "throw," and ten dollars per night. Coca-colas were served for twenty-five cents, though they were a nickel everywhere else in town. Home brew could be had as well.

On one particular July 4, Mollie and her girls went into town dressed in white. Matching black horses with white harnesses pulled the Victoria carriage as the dapper driver, dressed in a white suit, guided the vehicle around town for a little advertising. When they entered their carriage into the July 4 float contest, jealous wives informed their husbands that if Madam Mollie won first prize due to their vote, they need not come home that night. Someone else was declared the winner.

Several times every year, Mollie's sportin' house was raided by the police. The community was happy, police collected fees, the girls were examined by local doctors and then it was back to business as usual. But one night there was a fire at Mollie's house, and after the volunteer firefighters quickly extinguished the blaze, they were invited to rest a little while and perhaps enjoy the appreciation of Mollie and her beautiful girls. Of course, that turned out to be one of the nights the police decided to raid the bawdy house, and all of the firefighters were arrested. In protest, they resigned from the volunteer fire department, leaving much of the city unprotected. Charges were dropped, apologies were exchanged and accepted and the city was safe from fire once again.

In 1899, at the age of forty-seven, Mollie Teal died. Some historians believe her death was the result of a chronic case of venereal disease. Perhaps she was aware of her impending death as well. Her last will and testament was written and signed on July 31, 1898.

Mollie would not be forgotten any time soon. Her will included instructions that her house be left for a friend, Mollie Greenleaf, during her life. Upon Miss Greenleaf's death, it would go to the City of Huntsville "for the use and benefit of the white public schools, or for a City Hospital as the City authorities may elect." Her assets would be liquidated, and money would be used to buy books for a library or some other use in the public schools. Shortly after her death, however, a claim for her estate was entered into by someone named John Smith, allegedly an heir, and others who were not identified. After several rulings, the terms of her will were upheld, with the exception of two bank accounts that were not specified in her list of assets. The money in those accounts went to John Smith and others.

Miss Greenleaf lived only a few years, and upon her death, the building was remodeled and opened as an infirmary. Those who worked in the infirmary remembered that at times the screen door would seem to close by itself and hook. They laughed and joked that Mollie was there to make sure that everyone behaved properly. Whatever the case, Mollie's legacy led to the establishment of one of the finest medical facilities in the state of Alabama, ensuring that she would not be forgotten. For many years, a large portrait of Mollie was displayed in the lobby. Today, no one knows where that portrait is. The home eventually burned.

In the meantime, she was buried next to her mother, Mary Smith, who died when Mollie was only nineteen. Yet another mystery persists. Every two weeks or so, someone would bring flowers to Mollie's grave. A PVC pipe cut to about six inches was installed next to her headstone as a makeshift flower vase. The mystery was, for the most part, unnoticed by the residents of Huntsville, except to a few. For reasons unknown, the flowers stopped appearing at Mollie's grave in the fall of 2007—108 years after her death.

THE LAST WORD

The Jonestown cult suicides attracted worldwide attention in the late fall of 1978, but when a Huntsville woman saw her son's body in one of the pictures of the tragedy, she vowed not to rest until his body was returned to Huntsville for burial. She paid for a grave site and bought a tombstone, but for years, questions remained about who was actually buried in the Maple Hill Cemetery plot.

This story begins on November 18, 1978, thousands of miles away. Reverend Jim Jones ordered the execution and suicide of over nine hundred people in the Jonestown commune near Guyana in South America. In the weeks that followed, the world learned details of the charismatic madman who started the People's Temple in Northern California. Jones brainwashed some twenty thousand people and convinced them to turn over their worldly possessions and follow him to a secluded nirvana, which he egotistically named for himself. Jim Jones, the former director of the San Francisco Housing Authority, resigned his post under a dark cloud of controversy to build a society that would relegate everyone to the same social status. Their sacrifices, in the meantime, netted him millions of dollars in property and cash.

When former members reported cases of abuse, people held against their will and others who were killed if they disobeyed Jones, California congressman Leo Ryan, along with an entourage of newsmen, went on a fact-finding trip to Jonestown. Once there, nine cult members pleaded with Ryan to take them back to California. As they loaded into the small plane to return to the States, one cult member pulled out a gun and opened fire.

Truckloads of other cult members swiftly drove in from their hiding places in the jungle to finish off the attack. Congressman Ryan was killed, along with four other people.

Jones and the People's Temple were now threatened. Soon there would be police all around and Jones would go to prison. In a ritualistic act that had been rehearsed many times before, Jones ordered that everyone drink poison-laced punch. Parents were instructed to give it to their children before ingesting it themselves. There was evidence, however, that not everyone was willing to swallow the poison—their bullet wounds were not self-inflicted.

Among the millions of people who turned the pages of *Life* magazine to look at the gruesome pictures was Huntsville nurse Marjorie Balisok. To her horror, she recognized the lifeless faces of her son, Jerry, and his wife. She recognized the shirt on the body—it was one she had bought for him herself.

The road that led Jerry Balisok to Jonestown was no less strange than the surreal deaths of over nine hundred people. As a youth, he had an interest in motorcycles and decided to open a motorcycle shop sometime after high school. His widowed mother took out a second mortgage on her Pansy Street home. Though at first the business seemed to do well, Jerry soon found himself unable to meet the financial obligations associated with owning a business. As the business began to slip, Jerry started to write bad checks.

It didn't take long for the authorities to learn of his financial creativity, and he was indicted on thirteen separate counts of forgery. Rather than face the charges and possible jail time, Jerry left town with his wife and family. A fugitive warrant was issued for his arrest.

Through phone records and credit card bills, the authorities were able to trace Jerry and his family to Miami and the Bahamas, but because they could not find his exact location, they were unable to make an arrest. In December 1977, Jerry called his mother for the last time. He told her that he was heading to South America with a new identity.

Marjorie Balisok was not an outgoing person. She was remembered by a former employee of Big Springs Café, which was at that time located near the Russel Erskine Hotel. Marjorie rode her bicycle to the café every morning for breakfast on her way to work and stopped again for supper on her way home. She was polite but did not go out of her way to get to know people. All of that changed when she lost her son.

Mrs. Balisok wanted her son's body back home for burial. Every move she made, however, seemed to be frustrated by government bureaucracy.

In these years before DNA testing, government officials were understandably reluctant to release a body without absolute positive identification. Because the bodies had bloated in the hot sun, exacerbated by the effects of the poison, their condition made it almost impossible to identify them. No one seemed willing to take a mother's word.

Mrs. Balisok was notified that Jerry's body might be released to another family. She intensified her efforts by firing off letters to Senator Howell Heflin, numerous federal officials and news reporters. A 1980 story in the *Huntsville Times* ran the picture she identified, as well as the heartbreak of her struggle. She even suggested that her son's picture be shown to Jonestown survivors to prove that he was there. Her request was denied on the grounds that officials felt it might be construed as harassment. She was denied help everywhere she turned. Many people, including Senator Heflin, wondered how anyone could possibly be identified in the blurry photograph.

Living in a small apartment on Brandon Street, Marjorie Balisok became an expert on the events of the Jonestown Massacre, as well as the life of Jim Jones. Her son had once called her from Puerto Rico asking for a sum of money that coincided with the amount required by Jim Jones to become a member of his cult. She had already been warned by federal officials not to help him elude authorities in any way. In her research, Mrs. Balisok was able to tie Jim Jones to business dealings in Puerto Rico, establishing yet another connection between her son and the cult leader.

It was suggested by some officials that Mrs. Balisok wanted to have her son declared dead so that charges against him would be dropped. Was this some elaborate and convenient scheme to keep him out of jail? She said that she would have preferred to see him alive and in prison, but there was no doubt in her mind that Jerry was dead. The insurance policies in his name would have been only enough to cover his burial expenses—it certainly wasn't a grand scheme to collect insurance money.

Mrs. Balisok took her cause to wherever she could get public interest and support. She was interviewed by several publications over the years, and many wondered how she could be so certain that Jerry was involved in the Jim Jones cult. In her extensive research, she also must have learned that Jim Jones appealed to people who drifted in no apparent direction. In one interview, she said that Jonestown was the only place her son could go.

Mrs. Balisok's tenacity drew the attention of several other interested agencies. Jerry owed American Express $10,000, along with the many people who had received his bad checks. They were as certain that he was alive as

Mrs. Balisok was that he was dead. Without positive proof of his death, they wanted the case kept open.

Victims of the Jonestown Massacre were taken to Dover, Maryland, for possible identification. Because of decomposition, many could not be identified and were taken to Oakland, California, for burial in a common grave some six months later. According to a local acquaintance, Marjorie was in California waiting when the victims' bodies were removed from the plane; her intention was to intercept her son's body and bring him home for burial. She was determined. She told officials at Dover that her son "wasn't much of a person, but he was my son. I want his body so I can bury him."

After endless struggles, there seemed to be closure to the case. In a final act of love, she had a monument placed over his plot at Maple Hill Cemetery. Bitter and angry at the authorities who seemed to put roadblocks in her path, she had her frustrations carved into the headstone. The words "Damn the State Dept." serve as a reminder to everyone of a woman's determination to have the last word.

Satisfied that Jerry Balisok was dead, the authorities dropped the outstanding charges against him. A few years later, on May 23, 1983, confident that she had done all she could for her son, Marjorie Balisok finally found the peace that had eluded her in life. She died and was buried next to her son's plot. On the warm spring day of her funeral, men who had never known Marjorie Balisok were among the mourners. FBI agents mingled in the crowd, hopeful that Jerry Balisok would come to say one final farewell to his mother. He was not there.

The story might have ended there if not for a phone call to local police in 1989 asking for information about Jerry Balisok. He was presumed dead, the Huntsville authorities answered, but that was not the case. He was in jail in Seattle, Washington.

The story quickly unfolded. In the 1970s, Jerry and his family had moved to Renton, Washington, where he assumed the identity of a man named Ricky Wetta. Jerry, aka Ricky, had worked at several places, including Boeing Company, and had been fired from one job when it was discovered that he had lied on his employment application. Unbelievably, he claimed to have been a graduate of Cambridge University.

Jerry then drifted into one investment scheme or another until his 1989 arrest for shooting Emmett Thompson in Seattle, Washington. In spite of being shot three times in the back of the head and once in the arm while they were supposedly doing target practice in the woods, Thompson had survived. Thompson told King County Police that Wetta wanted him dead because he knew of Wetta's plot to have his Wenatchee hotel burned for the insurance money. Wetta's claim that he shot Thompson in self-defense when Thompson threatened him with a knife was unconvincing, and he was charged with attempted murder.

Ricky Wetta's fingerprints were run through the FBI database when it was suspected that he was using an alias. The FBI made the startling discovery that the man held in charges of attempted murder was Huntsville's own Jerry Balisok. The real Ricky Wetta was living in Florida.

On March 9, 1990, amended charges were filed against him in King County Superior Court, naming him as Jerry Balisok. On April 9, 1990, a King County, Washington jury found Jerry Balisok guilty of attempted murder in the first degree, with criminal intent. He was given a twenty-year sentence and fined $530.02. Although he appealed the verdict, it was upheld on February 14, 1994.

So who is buried in Maple Hill Cemetery under the tombstone intended for Jerry Balisok? No one. The grave is empty. In spite of Marjorie Balisok's determination, she was never able to convince authorities that it was her son's body in the picture in *Life* magazine.

In Huntsville's peaceful and beautiful Maple Hill Cemetery is a gravestone that causes more than a few curious people to wonder about the story behind the strange words and remember the actions of a madman in the late fall of 1978. But for all the evil that Jim Jones inspired, this is one event he cannot claim credit for.

Jerry Bibb Balisok
Born Sept. 8, 1955
Murdered in Guyana, Nov. 13, 1978
Buried in Oakland Cal. May 1979
DAMN THE STATE DEPT.

THE HIGH SHERIFF OF
LIMESTONE COUNTY

One spring morning, two visitors walked into the Limestone County sheriff's office for an appointment with Sheriff Mike Blakely. A well-heeled man and woman stood in the far corner of the reception room, away from the others. They looked nervous, and they were not of the "I brung Bubba some cigarettes down to the jail" crowd.

"Sheriff says he'll be here directly," the dispatcher said, with not the least bit of excitement in her voice. "There's been a bank robbery."

"What bank was it?" one visitor asked.

"Reliance, I believe," the dispatcher answered.

"Long as it wasn't my bank, I'm OK."

Within minutes, Sheriff Mike Blakely skidded into the jail with his straw cowboy hat slung low over his face and two paper sacks in his hand. He turned to the two professional-looking people in the corner of the lobby, handed them the bags filled with cash and told them that the suspect had robbed the bank with a BB gun. Ah, yes—the nervous Nellies were bank employees. "You can use the conference room to count up your money. Come on," he said to the visitors, "It's lunchtime and I'm hungry."

Another day in the world of law enforcement.

Sheriff Blakely was matter-of-fact about the episode, as if it were something that happened quite often in Athens, Alabama. It was a rare occurrence, actually, but in twenty-seven years as sheriff of Limestone County, he had seen it all, heard it all and been in the middle of it all. The bank robber was stopped when a spike strip was laid across the road during the pursuit. When the robber stepped out of his car, a piece of paper fell out onto the pavement. "Put your money in the sack. I've got two people waiting outside. Don't do anything stupid and no one will get hurt." Yep, this case was open and shut.

Mike Blakely knew from the time he was in high school that he wanted to be in law enforcement. He had the personality of a politician, something he was born with, and a good foundation of common sense. He watched and learned from others and never lost his sense of humor, even in times of great tragedy and danger. But what he liked the most was living every day on the edge and the excitement of the unknown. He was a rompin', stompin' adrenaline junkie.

In the last two-plus decades, many changes have come about in the crime industry. More crimes are drug related. Whether the suspects buy or sell drugs, steal to support a drug habit or murder while under the influence of drugs, their crimes can all be traced back to a single common denominator.

In June 1988, Mike was working on an undercover drug operation. Amanda and Stanley were both busted for drugs, but Mike wanted to get the source, and they agreed to help capture their dealer, Townsend, in return for leniency in their own crimes. A body microphone was attached to Stanley, concealed in his San Diego Chargers ball cap, and they were given "flash money" to purchase five pounds of marijuana. They would meet up with Townsend, and as soon as the deal could be made, the arrest would take place. But no matter how much planning goes into an operation, there are always ways it can go wrong. Townsend told them that he would drive them up into Tennessee to see *his* dealer.

The sheriff had no jurisdiction in Tennessee, and he needed for them to make the deal in Alabama. So he told Amanda and Stanley to explain that there were outstanding warrants for their arrest in Tennessee and that they would not take the risk of going to jail. Townsend understood, put them in the car and drove to a secluded spot, where they would wait outside for him to get his own dealer to come to them. Amanda and Stanley were instructed to make small talk about where they were going, where the car was turning and so forth in order for Mike to lay back without being spotted but not lose them altogether.

As Amanda and Stanley waited on Burnt Schoolhouse Road for the dealer to return, Mike backed his GMC Jimmy over a hill and concealed it in the weeds. With him was a Channel 19 news reporter ready to catch the whole deal on camera. Amanda smoked a cigarette and drank from a SunDrop can as they waited. Just down the road was another vehicle with two reserve officers to block the road in case they tried to escape. Before long, Townsend returned in his truck, followed by a sedan. Harold Dover, the Tennessee dealer, saw the money and left. He returned shortly, got out of his sedan and presented a five-pound hunk of marijuana on the tailgate of the truck. Sheriff Blakely busted out from his hiding place brandishing a 9mm machine gun. Townsend took off in the field as Sheriff Blakely lunged at Dover. Before he could react, Dover was subdued. It looked like the whole event was neatly tied up until Harold's son, Jason, suddenly sat up in his father's car, where he had been concealed, and opened fire with a shotgun.

The reserve officers were now on the scene. Blakely had Harold Dover in front of him as a shield and was firing his machine gun. With Dover struggling and flailing, he couldn't get a clear shot. In the meantime, Jason Dover shattered the backup's windshield and shot reserve officer Buddy Van Dyke in both legs. They returned fire, hitting Townsend's truck, with Blakely and Harold Dover on the other side. Blakely had a chokehold on Dover and tried to return fire by shooting under the truck, but his machine gun jammed. He tried to eject the clip but gave up, dropped the 9mm and grabbed his service revolver instead.

At the sound of the first shots, Amanda and Stanley lit out, headed for cover. Video of the event showed Amanda bounding across the field on her long legs. Later on, as they watched the whole scene on video, they all laughed. As Amanda ran for her very life, she took a drag from her cigarette and a swig from her SunDrop without slowing down!

Jason Dover surrendered, but the struggle with his father was not over. Sheriff Blakely was still grappling with Harold Dover, and as one of the reserve officers jumped over the truck to help, Dover managed to grab the 9mm machine gun and point it directly at the reserve officer's belly. He pulled the trigger repeatedly, but luckily Sheriff Blakely's efforts to disengage the clip had worked and the gun would not fire. Needless to say, Harold Dover was forcefully subdued.

Sheriff Blakely drove around for an hour looking for Amanda and Stanley until he found them about a mile away, out of breath and scared to death. Townsend got away, but not for long. He was later captured in Atlanta. Harold Dover got life in prison with no parole, while his son got leniency because of his age. Reserve Officer Buddy Van Dyke survived, but his wife refused to let him ride with Sheriff Blakely again.

On another occasion, Blakely stopped someone on Highway 99 and found a small amount of marijuana and $360 cash. Even though it was a small amount, the guy was out on parole, and he was looking at more jail time. Sheriff Blakely told the driver that he knew he was going to buy more drugs, so he offered him a deal: set up a drug deal with his dealer and he would get leniency in return.

As it turned out, his drug dealer, a man named Mason, was out on parole for murder. Sheriff Blakely knew the guy well. He had gone to his home to arrest him one day and had him in cuffs when Mason's phone rang. Mason was allowed to answer the phone. He told the caller he wasn't able to talk because he was "all tied up." It was quite the understatement. Mason's wife was also known to smoke great quantities of marijuana.

The suspect called his dealer, Mason, and told him his tire was flat (Sheriff Blakely had let the air out of one tire). "Bring the drugs here and tools to help me fix my tire," he said, "and I won't need to go to your place. By the way, I'll be wanting more than we talked about."

It didn't work that way of course. Mason picked the man up, took him to his trailer and made the deal. The sheriff hadn't witnessed the transaction, and it wouldn't stand in court. Sheriff Blakely went to Mason and bluffed, telling him that the serial numbers on the money he had just taken were recorded and they had him for selling drugs.

Still another deal was about to be made. The sheriff told him he'd get leniency by setting up a sting operation for Mason's dealer. The delivery would be made the following morning at ten o'clock at Mason's trailer. The next morning, with everyone early and in place, Mason was instructed to scratch his head when the deal had been completed. But when the dealer from Iron City, Tennessee, drove up, his wife and kids were in the car with him, leaving law enforcement with an unexpected kink in their slinkies. He got out and went inside Mason's trailer and Mason followed him inside. Now what?

After what seemed like a very long time, Mason's son came out of the trailer, scratching his head. Then his daughter came out of the trailer, scratching her head. Mason's wife then came out, and like the others, she was scratching her head. To a bystander, it looked like the whole family had a bad case of lice!

But what happened next would be told over and over for many years to come. Blakely's backup investigator was coached to make it look like Mason was going down in the drug bust as well. Mason was paranoid and worried that, as a snitch, there would be retaliation. When the arrest commenced, Mason would run off around the trailer and the investigator would chase him, firing in the air and yelling for Mason to surrender. They all moved in, and Sheriff Blakely got the Iron City dealer without a struggle. Blakely had his .45 pointed in the drug dealer's ear as he cuffed him. Just as they had discussed, Mason took off running with the investigator in hot pursuit. But instead of firing his pistol in the air, for whatever reason the investigator yelled, at the top of his lungs, "Bam! Bam!"

Had he actually yelled "Bam, Bam"? Sheriff Blakely could hardly control his laughter. The arrest was made, but Sheriff Blakely made sure that the investigator never lived it down.

Other incidents were not at all funny. Though common sense would tell you that alcohol and firearms don't mix, there are those who have to prove it. And all too often, it is the last thing they do. Such was the case when a man on East Limestone Road started drinking and grabbed his shotgun for reasons unknown. He chased his family out of the house, and when an officer was called to the scene, the drunk chased him off too. The officer called for backup.

The hours wore on, and the man kept drinking and threatening. The neighbors were evacuated for their safety in case of stray bullets. The drunk man's anger began to escalate, and he swore that he'd take out all the cops he could before taking his own life. As long as everyone was far enough away not to be seriously injured by shotgun pellets, they could wait. But when the drunk's wife told Sheriff Blakely there were high-powered rifles inside the trailer, the tone changed. The drunk took a baseball bat and starting busting out windows in the trailer and his truck. He continued to drink, and continued to holler. His brothers came and tried to talk him into giving up, but he threatened them as well. Strangely enough, the brothers brought beer with them to drink, too.

A sniper was poised and ready to take the drunk out if the situation got deadly. Just then, the drunk uttered, in Sheriff Blakely's terms, the last words of a redneck: "Hey! Watch this!"

He swung around and pointed his shotgun directly at the deputies. Sheriff Blakely gave the signal to the sniper. The rest seemed to happen in slow motion. A bullet ripped through the front side of the drunk and out the back side. Sheriff Blakely ran across the field and lunged at the rifle in case the drunk reached for it. But he was already dead. Unbelievably, the brothers of the now dead man reacted in a way that no one could have predicted. One of them took his false teeth out of his mouth and threw them onto the ground. He threw his beer can at the sheriff and came after him. It didn't progress further than that.

Still, one has to ask, why pull out his false teeth and throw them down before coming after the sheriff? As Sheriff Blakely explains, in a rather matter-of-fact tone, he had once tangled with the guy and it cost him some teeth.

And then there was the saga of Edna and Reuben. Edna was a tall, big-boned woman. She was married to a dried-up little man named Reuben who drank to excess. When he was over the top, he abused Edna verbally and threatened to kill her. Edna approached Sheriff Blakely and told him her woes. "What do I do?" she asked.

"I'd shoot him!" Blakely said, tongue-in-cheek.

But there comes a time in everyone's life when we wish we could take our words back, and that time surely came for Sheriff Blakely. One Sunday morning, Edna attached a tape recorder under the kitchen table and let it run. Reuben was drunk, hung over or both. What transpired was caught entirely on tape.

"Would you like to go to church with me?" Edna asked Reuben innocently. The tirade began. He started in on her, cussing and stomping. She wouldn't let it go. "Cook you some breakfast?"

He was just getting wound up. He let go of another string of profanity. But Edna didn't stop there. She knew exactly what buttons to push, and her timing was flawless. She delivered the final *coup de grâce* that sent him over the edge: "You want me to go in there on the bed and let you lay down on top of me?"

"I shoulda killed you way back when, you sorry old $#@#$$! I oughta get my gun and blow you away, you $#@#$$!" On and on he continued.

There were muffled sounds, as if a struggle was taking place, complete with lots of teeth gnashing and plenty more profanity. Suddenly, two shots were fired. The next sound was Edna throwing open the door, yelling, "Hep! Hep! Somebody call the po-lice! I done shot Reuben!" One can only imagine the scene at that point: Edna threw the .22 pistol to the ground and ran out, hands flailing in the air, screaming to high heaven.

Sheriff Blakely got the call, and his first thought was the conversation he had with Edna when he tossed out the words "I'd shoot him."

What have I done? he thought to himself, hoping that Reuben was alive, that Edna wouldn't repeat what he said, that he wouldn't spend the rest of his life as some prisoner's girlfriend.

As it turned out, Reuben was only grazed in the temple by the bullet, though he bled profusely, giving the impression that it was much worse. When one of the deputies found him, he had staggered outside, more from the influence of alcohol than from a gunshot wound, and had dropped his overalls down around his ankles to answer the call of nature by the side of the road.

Ultimately, Reuben died, but not with any help from Edna. And it was years later.

In a small town, one gets to know the regular scofflaws and miscreants. They become guests of the county from time to time, get a few good meals, maybe get dried out and are then sent on their merry way. One such regular, another who enjoyed his liquor a little too well, happened to take pride in thoroughly cleaning and detailing the sheriff's truck whenever he was incarcerated. He always called the sheriff "Sheriff Blakely" or "Mr. Mike." The sheriff appreciated his hard work, and whenever he was there, the prisoner waited by the front desk for Blakely to toss him his truck keys when he came in so he could drive it around back and get to work on it. One morning, Blakely came in and saw that his truck-cleaning guest was there.

"Good morning, Mike," the prisoner said as he snatched the keys in midair. Blakely started around the corner and then stopped dead in his tracks.

"Stop…right…there!" Something wasn't right. The prisoner hadn't called him "Mr. Mike," and he hadn't called him "Sheriff Blakely." He called him "Mike." The sheriff relieved him of the keys and had him take the breathalyzer test. Sure enough, he was still drunk.

Sheriff Blakely laments that criminals these days have no class at all. Too many are committing crimes to feed drug habits and don't care what they do or who they hurt. One woman, also a frequent guest in the jail, had a shoplifting habit. Caroline could hide a television and a twenty-pound turkey at the same time. Occasionally she would get careless and end up answering to the Law. She would spend a little time in jail, get some good food in her, put on some much-needed weight and then head back out, looking to steal something for her kids and her drug habit. She had a sense of humor about her, though, and once saw Sheriff Blakely walking on the far side of the courthouse square. She hollered out after him, "Sheriff! You better send me some money for these kids! Don't you look at me like that, you know good and well these are your kids! They's hungry and need clothes and shoes!" Caroline got what she wanted—Sheriff Blakely was mortified and embarrassed.

After twenty-seven years on the job, Sheriff Blakely has seen it all. Though he can no longer kick down a door on the first try or wrestle some grizzly bear of a criminal to the ground like he did in days gone by, he's done more than his fair share of it and still enjoys being in the middle of it all. Every day is a new challenge, and everybody processes experiences and reacts to them in their own unique way.

The conversation turns back to the bank robbery, although it wasn't the only incident of the morning. A woman of questionable sanity had been picked up and brought back to the jail. She stripped her own clothing off, and what happened next can only be described using the words of a female employee, who also happens to be a minister, as she started inside the cell to deal with the prisoner: "I might oughtta be calling HazMat on this one," she said as she pulled rubber gloves over her hands and took a deep breath. "Get the mace ready, I'm a-GOING in! That woman has done doo-dooed all over her cell!"

FULL CIRCLE

Occasionally, a story emerges that defies the boundaries of one's imagination. This is one such case. The grisly discovery of Nell Griffin's body attracted the grim attention of the entire city of Huntsville. It involved the longest trial up to that time, and the courtroom was packed with spectators every day. After the seats were all gone, curious onlookers filled the aisles. The murderer's mother testified that she marked the time on the night of the murder by the beginning of her favorite television show, *Twilight Zone*. Yet before the trial ended, it could have made for an episode of that show itself.

Late on the evening of Sunday, March 21, 1971, a call was received at the Huntsville Fire Department about a grass fire in a wooded area near 905 Kennamer Drive in Huntsville. The call came in at 10:43 p.m. from a doctor who was driving home. When members of the Huntsville Fire Department arrived, they discovered that it wasn't a grass fire. Instead, they found the nude body of a woman engulfed in flames near a swimming pool. It appeared that she had been doused with a flammable liquid, and by the time firefighters arrived, her body had been almost completely consumed. In the woods nearby were several items of clothing, a ripped pantsuit and a bloody and broken necklace.

Huntsville police were called to the scene, and an investigation began immediately. One of the Kennamer Drive neighbors heard what sounded like a screaming woman at about 10:15 p.m. and then the sound of a car spinning out on loose gravel. The victim was identified as Iva Nell Griffin, a forty-two-year-old attractive strawberry blonde employee of General

Electric. Mrs. Griffin, a native of Fort Payne, Alabama, lived in an apartment located at 919 Minor Street in Huntsville.

Earlier that same evening, Nell and her neighbor, Kay Freeman, were drinking at the Hickory House Lounge and eventually decided to go to the Carousel Club on University Drive. The lounge featured live music on most nights, and couples danced through the fog of cigarette smoke that drifted through the darkened club. In the dim light, couples groped each other and flirted on the dance floor, some looking for temporary affection and others for long-term companionship.

At about 6:00 p.m., a tall, dark-haired man approached the ladies' table. Ronald Lee Martz, age thirty-two, struck up a conversation with the women, but it soon became clear that he was interested in Nell Griffin, a divorcée. They talked quietly among themselves, kissed a few times and then danced. At about 7:00 p.m., Kay Freeman decided to leave after feeling very much in the way. Kay told Nell that she would call a taxi to pick her up and take her home, but Nell insisted that Kay take her car and handed her the keys. Kay indicated that she might go back to the Hickory House Lounge.

Just after 11:30 p.m., as members of the Huntsville Fire Department were putting out the fire, Ronald Martz was being arrested by police officers Butch Wyatt and Don Sadler for driving drunk. He had driven his car off Maysville Road. Officer Sadler saw a woman's purse and coat in the car, as well as an empty gasoline can. He noticed that the purse straps were broken and part of a strap was missing. At that time, police knew of no connection between Martz and Nell Griffin. Martz's car was towed to Bridge's Texaco on Oakwood Avenue, and the driver called Martz's father to pay the towing bill. He refused.

The next morning, Kay Freeman got a telephone call from two people who knew Nell, asking if she had any idea where Nell was. They had heard a news report that a body had been found and somehow thought it might be Nell. Kay said she had heard on the news about a burning body, but no name was mentioned. In the meantime, Officer J.C. Brooks had picked up Ronald Martz at his father's Oakwood Avenue home, where he also lived, to come in to the station to answer questions about the body that had been discovered. Investigators asked to see Martz's clothing from the night before and found on his pants suspicious stains that appeared to be blood.

According to Martz, he had been with a woman the night before but did not know her name. He said that they left the club at about 8:00 p.m., when she agreed to go up on Monte Sano Mountain to "make out." They got into an argument on the way, and when they got to the Five Points area, she jumped out of the car while he was still driving.

State Toxicologist Vann Pruitt took the clothing retrieved from Ronald Martz and found Type O and Type A blood, consistent with the victim (Type O) and the accused murderer (Type A). The toxicologist also discovered that Nell Griffin had died as the result of hemorrhaging from a lacerated liver caused by a massive blow to the abdomen. She could have been punched or stomped. Among the items of clothing and other articles retrieved from the murder scene was a purse strap that matched the one found in Martz's car. The evidence was more than convincing that Ronald Martz had caused the death of Nell Griffin.

Ronald Martz was indicted for murder, and the trial was set for later that same year. Judge Tom Younger presided over the trial, which began in October 1971. The jury was sequestered during the trial. Attorney Richard Kempaner, who was hired to defend Ronald Martz, did not want the gruesome photographs of Mrs. Griffin's burned body shown to the jury. District Attorney Fred Simpson and his assistant prosecutor, Bart Lofton, wanted them admitted into evidence for exactly the same reason—the shocking nature of the pictures would remain in the jury members' minds. Judge Younger said that he would take the matter under consideration. He later agreed to let the pictures be shown to the jury. Another round of arguments ensued when Kempaner asked witnesses about the men Nell had been out with, to the objection of the prosecutor, who accused him of smearing the victim's name. Kempaner indicated that he was trying to show that Nell knew and had dated many men and that perhaps a jealous boyfriend, or another man, had killed her.

One of the many men Nell Griffin was alleged to have been involved with was Chuck Clark, a married man who was supposedly very jealous of anyone Nell drank or danced with. Five months before her death, he was overheard telling her that if he saw her on the dance floor again, he would "stomp the hell out of you." In a strange subplot, Dot Warden, Clark's wife, took the witness stand and said that she was working in Indiana at the time of the murder and that Clark had driven to Indiana and asked her to provide an alibi for the night of the murder. Her reliability was discredited, however, when Judge John Green found out that she was in town. He had her put in jail for contempt of court for an incident in a previous domestic case. Dot Warden had an axe to grind with her ex-husband.

It was also suggested by Kempaner that the pantsuit Nell was wearing the night she was murdered was given to her by Chuck Clark. In her purse was a note with several words written on it, including Chuck's name. The words "trust, truthfulness, understanding, sharing, companionship, kindness" made no sense to anyone but, apparently, the victim.

On Wednesday, October 13, a surprise witness was called for the defense. Mike Marlowe, a Huntsville firefighter, testified that when he arrived at the scene of Mrs. Griffin's burning body, he heard a cough somewhere behind him. He thought it was another firefighter, Leroy Collette, but Collette said it wasn't him. The defense attorney hoped to show that the real killer was still at the scene and therefore it couldn't have been Martz. Dewey Lehman, another firefighter, was later called to the stand. He testified that he was the one who had coughed.

Ronald Martz's mother testified that her son came home at 10:30 p.m. the night of the murder. She remembered distinctly that she was watching her favorite television show, *Twilight Zone*. Her testimony was discredited, however, when police records indicated that Martz was arrested at 11:34 p.m.

On Thursday, October 14, Ron Martz took the stand to testify in his own defense. He said that he and Nell Griffin drove around for awhile, but he began to get paranoid when he noticed a police car following him. Nell panicked at some point, and they got into an argument. She tried to jump from the moving car while Martz was still driving. He hit her in the face with the back of his hand and pulled her down into the seat until he could stop the car. When he took his hand off of her, she flew out of the car and ran across the street and away from him. He did not see her again after that. He claimed that when the police arrested him for driving drunk, he was on his way to the Hickory House Lounge, where Nell Griffin's car was parked, so he could give her back her purse. He also attempted to explain the presence of the gasoline can. He said he had taken his son fishing that day and thought he would be able to rent a boat. However, the gasoline can was empty.

Closing arguments began on Thursday, October 14. The prosecution asked for the death penalty. Defense Attorney Richard Kempaner argued that it could have been any one of a number of people who knew Nell that could have killed her. He also said there was nothing but circumstantial evidence against his client—not enough to morally convict someone of murder. District Attorney Fred Simpson said that the strategy used by Kempaner was to discredit those involved in the investigation and blame everyone but Martz, even Santa Claus, for the victim's death.

At 4:20 p.m. on October 14, the trial was handed over to the jury for deliberation. After six hours, it recessed for the night. On Friday, October 15, members of the jury, eleven men and one woman, met again to come to an agreement. At 11:00 a.m., the jury announced it had reached a verdict. The jury found Ronald Martz guilty of second-degree murder and gave him twenty years in prison.

After the trial was over, it was revealed that Mrs. Griffin was afraid she would die of cancer within the year. She had already had one breast removed because of cancer and had found lumps in her other breast.

In 1974, an appeal was made to the Supreme Court of Alabama for a new trial for Ronald Martz, but it was the opinion of the court that there was no reversible error made in the trial.

The story of Nell Griffin's death would take yet another bizarre turn. In 1977, Ronald Martz was paroled from prison. By the summer of 1979, he was working as a steelworker in Birmingham and had come to visit his family in Huntsville. On Friday, July 13, he was standing in a wading pool in the backyard of his parents' home on Oakwood Avenue. At about 4:45 a.m., his screams woke members of his family, who ran outside to find that Martz had doused himself with gasoline and lit a fire that engulfed him in flames. The fire was put out, leaving him with burns on over 60 percent of his body. He had apparently put a gag in his mouth and around his neck, according to the burn pattern around his face, but it had slipped out and he screamed, while at the same time inhaling fire that severely damaged his lungs. It was ruled by detectives to be an attempted suicide, but he was not successful in taking his own life.

The manner of his attempted suicide calls for much speculation. Was he obsessed with fire? Did he feel it was a fitting penance for the death of Nell Griffin? Only Ronald Martz was capable of answering those questions.

AFTER THE GAME

Decatur resident Charles Ray Lovett, age twenty-nine, worked as a typesetter for the *Decatur Daily*. His wife of seven years worked part time at the local Dairy Queen, and they were the parents of six-year-old and fourteen-month-old sons. They lived at 806 Freemont Street, near the intersection of Eighth Street and Danville Road in Decatur. From all outward appearances, they had a solid marriage and no financial hardships. They seemed, even to their neighbors, to be the typical American family. A strange twist of fate would change all of that.

On October 2, 1969, Charles Ray Lovett attended a high school football game. The Austin Black Bears tied 20–20 with the Hartselle Tigers at Ogle Stadium. When the game ended, Mr. Lovett went out to the parking lot, but much to his surprise, his car was nowhere to be found. He got a ride to the police station to report it stolen. It appeared to be only a minor inconvenience, however. Before Lovett even knew his car was missing, Decatur police had apprehended Florida resident Glenn Dolvin shortly after he had hot-wired it and taken it for a joy ride.

Forty-year-old Glenn Dolvin already had an extensive criminal record. In 1957, a newspaper in Youngstown, Ohio, reported that Dolvin had been charged in the gangland-style death of Andrew Gerlach in Hubbard, Ohio. In the same year, he robbed the Boardman Branch of the Mahoning National Bank of $31,000 and was arrested several months later in San Diego with $18,500 as he tried to make a run to Mexico.

Unfortunately, he left Ohio and moved his criminal activity farther south. As a result of the theft of Charles Lovett's car, Dolvin was indicted on March

13, 1970, and charged with larceny. Charles Lovett was expected to testify at his trial, scheduled for later that year.

On Sunday, July 25, 1970, J.R. Garrett looked outside the plate-glass window of his barbershop in Decatur and saw a Cadillac pull up and park. It remained there for quite some time, but the driver did not get out of the car. Mr. Garrett watched until the car slowly pulled out and drove away. During the next week, Glenn Dolvin was seen walking around the area, which happened to be near Freemont Street, where the Lovett family lived. His manner was suspicious, and it was obvious he didn't belong there. He was trying not to be seen, making himself more obvious in the process. J.R. Garrett recognized him as the same man in the Cadillac, and he notified the police because he felt that Dolvin might be casing a nearby bank to plan a robbery. On August 16, Dolvin asked Rick Hames, who worked at a service station, for directions on how to find Freemont Street.

At 10:00 p.m. on Sunday, August 16, Charles Lovett called his wife at Dairy Queen just as they prepared to close. They spoke for a few minutes, and Charles asked her to bring him something to eat. After the call, Mrs. Lovett took the trash outside to the dumpster and saw a dark green Volkswagen parked next to her car in the parking lot. A man was in the driver's seat, and a woman sitting in the passenger's seat glared at her. Although it made her uncomfortable, she continued on to the dumpster. The car immediately left.

Fourteen-year-old Debbie Garrett was with her mother at the Handy Way convenience store on Ashley Drive, parallel to Freemont Street, late on the evening of August 16. She noticed a dark green Volkswagen idling in the parking lot with its headlights off. She watched as the car left the parking lot, turned slowly onto Freemont Street, still without headlights, and then returned to the parking lot where Handy Way was located. A few minutes later, the car again drove slowly onto Freemont Street. Shortly afterward, the Volkswagen came out of Freemont Street, but this time the headlights were on, the car was speeding and someone in the car screamed something she could not understand. As the car sped past, she noticed that a woman was driving and two men sat in the front seat with her.

At about the same time, Betty Third, a resident of Freemont Street, woke up to the sound of someone yelling for help. The time was 10:45 p.m. She heard a loud noise, a bang or a pop, and looked outside. A dark green Volkswagen drove slowly in front of her neighbors' house, the home of the Lovetts. A man walking next to her house turned over a barbecue grill belonging to her neighbor. She assumed that the pop she heard was the

Volkswagen back firing, and seeing that the man was gone, she went back to bed.

Mrs. Lovett arrived home at 11:05 p.m. She was surprised to find the front door of their home at 806 Freemont Drive wide open and the storm door ajar. Her husband's shoes and shirt were still laid out on the dresser for him to wear to work the next day, and the two children were soundly sleeping in their beds. There was no sign of a struggle, and so she assumed that he had stepped over to a neighbor's house for a chat. By 12:30 a.m., she had checked the yard and decided to call the Decatur Police Department. She was told to call back in an hour if he still hadn't returned. When she called back at 1:30 a.m., an investigation into his disappearance began. Police later searched the residence but found no fingerprints or bloodstains.

On August 16, 1970, Sue Dolvin, wife of Glenn Dolvin, was visited by Robert Hancock, an investigator with the Alabama Bureau of Investigation. Sue was living in Tamperick Trailer Park in Key West, Florida. Her dark green Volkswagen had an application for a new license plate taped onto the windshield, and a search of the car indicated that there were new floor mats. The car was impounded and searched by FBI agents, who found human blood on a cap, a brown paper sack and a map. Unfortunately, there was not enough blood to determine the type.

Sue Dolvin, who said she had married Glenn in Mexico in February 1970, was questioned about the August 16 disappearance of Charles Lovett. She said she had been in Florida all weekend, and her story could be corroborated by her brother in Bradenton, Florida, because he had called her over the weekend. Her brother, she explained, had been beaten in a fight and had been hospitalized for his wounds. Furthermore, she said she had gone to Bradenton with her husband from their Key West home. It was while they were in Miami on Tuesday, August 18, that a policeman pulled them over to inform them that their license plate was gone. After getting a temporary permit, they returned to their home in Key West.

The disappearance of Mr. Lovett did not change the status of the trial against Glenn Dolvin. He was convicted on November 10, 1970, of grand larceny, though he was a no-show for his trial. As it turned out, Dolvin had been arrested in Ohio for robbery and was serving time in an Ohio prison. He was extradited to Alabama to stand trial.

Sue Dolvin was arrested on November 11, 1970, and two witnesses, Mrs. Lovett and Debbie Garrett, identified her as the woman in the Volkswagen on August 16, 1970. Neither could positively identify Glenn Dolvin. Sue Dolvin made the statement that she had an alibi and knew nothing about a kidnapping. On November 20, Glenn and Sue were both indicted for the kidnapping of Charles Ray Lovett. Separate trials were held for the two of them in February 1971.

Sue Dolvin's alibi did not check out. An assistant director of the Manatee Memorial Hospital in Bradenton testified that Sue's brother had been in the hospital in September 1970 after a fight but not at all in August. A next-door neighbor in the trailer park testified that the Dolvins had been gone, along with their car, during the entire weekend. Another of Sue's claims was disproven. A teletype operator with the Florida Highway Patrol in Ocala, Florida, testified that at about midnight on August 17, a woman called to say that her license tag was missing from her car. Sue Dolvin told Clarence Lee Simpson that a gas station attendant in Ocala noticed it was gone and told her. When she arrived at the station shortly after her call, she was covered with dirt, her fingernails were dirty, there were smudges on her face and arms and she smelled like campfire smoke. Simpson understandably assumed that she had been camping at one of the nearby campgrounds. Sue Dolvin told Simpson they were on their way back to Alabama from Miami. A few days later, the lost tag was turned in to the Ocala Highway Patrol.

Both Sue and Glenn were convicted. Glenn received ten years in prison for kidnapping and an additional eight years for larceny in the theft of the automobile. But there was still no sign of Charles Lovett or his remains. A few years later, he was declared dead.

Fast forward. In Seminole County, Florida, three quarters of a mile from an interstate highway, a road construction firm was preparing a new roadbed in the Lake Mary area near Sanford. On December 7, 1977, a road scraper, operated by John C. Cardi, unearthed human remains. The skeleton was discovered under thirty inches of dirt on its back. The knees were up, and the arms and hands were crossed in the pelvic area. Taking these facts into consideration, it was improbable that the deceased had died of natural causes or suicide.

Dr. Joseph H. Davis, medical examiner for Dade County, examined the bones and decided that they belonged to a white adult man in or around his mid-twenties. Shotgun pellets and wadding were discovered around the skeleton, though Dr. Davis could not tell if the deceased had died from a gunshot wound or if he had been shot after his death. Dr. Richard Souviron, a forensic odontologist for over twelve years, looked at the teeth attached to the skull. He was able to determine that no teeth were missing, there were no cavities or fillings, they had not been cleaned and the deceased had been a smoker. Furthermore, they were unusually perfect—"a freak of nature," he described them—although there was evidence of periodontal disease. Mrs. Lovett confirmed that her husband's teeth were perfect, with no cavities and no fillings. She also said that he smoked two packs of cigarettes daily. Using a picture of Mr. Lovett taken in life while he was smiling, Dr. Souviron carefully compared the eight and a half teeth visible in the picture to the ones in the skull. In his opinion, they were an exact match, and the person in the picture and the skull were one and the same. His finding, arrived at in this unusual manner, was the first of its kind.

On May 4, 1978, forty-six-year-old Sue Anne Hamricka, a resident of Key West, Florida, was arrested for murder. She was also known as Sue Dolvin, wife of Glenn Dolvin. She had served her time for kidnapping and had been released from prison. Glenn Dolvin was also charged with murder. The assumption made by police, prosecutors and the jury was that Charles Lovett was kidnapped and murdered in order to keep him from testifying against Glenn and Sue Dolvin. It was not hard to arrive at that conclusion, considering Glenn Dolvin's criminal history and reputation as a professional thief.

On January 26, 1979, Glenn Dolvin was convicted of first-degree murder. The judgment was reversed on appeal, however, when it was ruled that his conviction was based on "speculation, suspicion, and conjecture."

Sue Dolvin was convicted of murder in the court of Judge Newton Powell. Attorney Jerry R. Knight filed her appeal for a new trial based on several errors. Through her attorney, Sue Dolvin objected to the manner in which the remains of Charles Lovett were identified—comparing a photo of him in life to the teeth of the skeleton. That objection was disallowed, in spite of the fact that it was an unusual method of identification, because it was ruled that Alabama case law supported the theory, as did Dr. Souviron's extensive and impressive credentials. Sue Dolvin objected to the judge's charge to the jury that it could infer malice and also requested a change of venue for a new trial, should it be granted, based on the newspaper publicity. There were other objections raised through her attorney, but ultimately her request for a new trial was turned down when it was ruled that she had received a fair trial.

The murder of Charles Lovett was a senseless crime—but aren't they all? Glenn Dolvin is rumored to be dead and his life of crime over. Sue Dolvin has been released from prison, and her whereabouts are unknown at this time. The family of Charles Lovett will continue to mourn his tragic murder for many years to come.

ABOUT THE AUTHOR

J acquelyn Procter Reeves is a native of Las Vegas, New Mexico, and a graduate of New Mexico Highlands University. She is the editor of North Alabama's *Valley Leaves* and associate editor of *Old Tennessee Valley* magazine in Decatur. Jacque is the curator of the historic Donnell House in Athens and owner of Avalon Tours in Huntsville. She conducts ghost walks, cemetery tours and historical tours and has served on Huntsville's Maple Hill Cemetery Stroll committee for some fourteen years. She teaches history to students all over the United States via distance learning through Early Works Museum in Huntsville. In her spare time, she has written scores of short stories and seven books and has served as a contributing writer to many other publications. Jacque lives in Huntsville.

Please visit us at
www.historypress.net